DRIVING
TECHNIQUES
For the Professional & Non Professional
4th Edition

By Anthony J. Scotti

PhotoGraphics Publishing

PhotoGraphics Publishing

23 Cool Water Court

Palm Coast, Florida 32137

386-246-3672, fax 386-445-7365

www.photographicspublishing.com

www.securitydriver.com

email: bestdives@hotmail.com

ISBN 13: 978-0-9793813-1-7

Library of Congress Control Number: 2007923729

Bisac: TRA001030, SC1041000, SP0000000

Driving Techniques © 2007 Anthony J. Scotti

"Shell" materials © Shell Oil Company

Bike Tips © Bike Florida and Florida's Share the Road Campaign, Lynda Lyle Moore

Edited by Claudia Sammartino, Gold Quill Ltd.

Cover Photo: © 2007 Galina Barsik/Dreamstime

Special Sales: This book is available at special discounts for schools and other bulk purchases. Call 386-246-3672 for pricing. Special editions, including personalized covers and corporate imprints, can be created in quantity for special uses.

Every effort has been made to ensure that the information in this book is correct, but the publisher, author and contributors do not assume, and hereby disclaim, liability to any party for loss or damage caused by errors or omissions.

Dedicated. . .
in loving memory of my wife *Judy*, and
to my daughter, *Toni-Ann*

About the Author

TONY SCOTTI

For the past 30 years, Tony Scotti has catered to the driver training needs of industry and public service agencies.

He has trained governments, corporations, law enforcement agencies and military organizations to protect themselves while in a vehicle. His clientele includes over 80% of the Fortune 100, police departments in twenty-two states, and a number of Federal agencies. He has trained more than 700 corporations in 33 countries on five continents.

Since 1974, he has grown to become the acknowledged leader in the highly specialized industry of high-risk driving. Many other training organizations adopted his training methods. He has conducted more programs in more locations than any other private training institution in the world. His name is synonymous with high-risk driving.

He has been the subject of numerous interviews in the national media, and has been a speaker at conferences throughout the world. He holds a B.S. in Engineering from Northeastern University.

Brief Contents

Detailed Contents

PART III — ACCIDENTS **211**

Chapter 22- **Accident Stats: Who, What, When, and How** 213

Chapter 23 - **What Causes Accidents?** **219**

Chapter 24 - **Typical Accident Scenarios: And How to Deal with Them** . . . **229**

List of Figures, Tables, and Boxes

FIGURES

TABLES

BOXES

See Index for a full list of
"DRIVING SCENARIOS"
(how to's and examples)

Author's Acknowledgments

I would like to thank the people that made this book possible.

First, there are the instructors of Tony Scotti Associates who did the research and the testing, and who spent many a day in God-forsaken hell-holes proving that all this theory actually works.

Then there is my daughter Toni Ann, who is my biggest critic and best friend, and who continues to prove the theory that the apple does not fall far from the tree. Poor kid.

Then there is Larry Snow. Larry did not actually help with the book, but he is married to my daughter and the kid deserves all the credit in the world.

I don't know what I can say about publisher Joyce Huber. Her persistence, patience, and understanding are what made this book possible. Without her there would be no book. May all those who choose to write have a Joyce Huber.

Special thanks to our editor, Claudia Sammartino; photographer, Jim Spencer; Dan Raber; consultant, Eleanor Eidson; Kathy Chiariello, Mercedes Benz Corporate Communications; Holly Hutchins, Shell Oil Company; Denise Wilkinson, Shell Oil Company; Tina Foley, The National Highway Traffic Safety Administration; Lyndy Lyle Moore, Bike Florida and Florida's Share the Road Campaign; and Bryan T. Sammartino, NJ Level II Fire Instructor.

Over the 30 years I have spent in the driver training/consulting business, I have worked and consulted with many top-notch specialists and drivers of all levels and abilities. Although there are too many to mention here individually, they — and the experiences we shared "in the trenches" — have enriched the pages of this book.

Introduction

THE "GOOD DRIVER" MYTH

A common misconception about driving is the definition of the "good driver."

Whether you drive for a living, live to drive, or just drive to get yourself around, if you think you're a "good driver" just because you can drive *fast,* you're sadly mistaken. Simply driving fast requires little skill if you're simply driving in a straight line. (Sure, professional drag racing drivers might differ with this evaluation, but that's a highly-specialized form of straight-line driving.)

Or you may think that your "maneuvering" skills are top notch if you routinely:

- Pass other cars when you please, without regard to safety
- Try to beat a yellow light
- Squeal tires every time you accelerate from a dead stop
- Weave through traffic
- Drive with one hand
- Cut people off in order to get ahead of them

People who regularly do this aren't "good" drivers, they're *aggressive and unsafe drivers.* They mistake *prudent caution* for timidity in driving. They mistake using their head before making a move as being timid — and they mistake fear for cowardice.

But, any racing driver will tell you that only *fools* take unnecessary chances on the road. *Caution* is the byword of racing — and it should be for *everyday* driving as well.

But prudent caution alone is not enough to make you a "good driver." There are several things you have to know and a lot you have to be able to do — and do consistently and intuitively — before you can call yourself a "good driver" — a safe driver.

- You have to know the rules of the road.

- You have to know your own physical and mental driving limitations.

- You have to know how to use, maintain, and control your vehicle properly.

- And you have to know how to handle the hazards and dangers that can crop up in the driving environment at any time.

Learning the basic rules of the road is the first step you should take.

BASIC RULES OF THE ROAD

Then ...

Seventy years ago, when there were few vehicles and roads were narrow, there were two simple traffic rules.

1. One required a driver to turn to the right when meeting a vehicle coming from the opposite direction.

2. The other required him to turn to the left when overtaking and passing a vehicle going in the same direction.

At other times, *a driver could use the center or any other part of the road.*

It is easy to imagine the confusion and wreckage that would result if these were the only rules followed today!

Figure I-1. The First Four-Wheel Car. Photo © Courtesy
Mercedes-Benz USA, LLC

And Now ...

**Today, rules of the road are standardized
throughout the United States to promote highway
safety.**

Any modifications will be normally indicated by traffic control
personnel or by signs or markings.

> **ALWAYS obey directions given by traffic control
> personnel or signs *regardless* of conflict with the
> general rules listed here.**

Although there are many rules to cover specific situations
(which we won't go into here), there are a few rules that apply
generally — and it is your responsibility as a "good" driver to
know them.

As you'll see, these rules are not that much different from the
rules of yore — but HOW you observe them on *today's* roads
with *today's* vehicles makes a big difference in whether you
have a safe trip or become a statistic.

So what are today's basic "rules of the road"?

> The following list is a brief outline, but we'll be looking *in detail* at   those listed — and the techniques for following them safely and legally — in the many chapters to come.

1. **Drive on the Right.** You must operate vehicles on the right of the highway, giving approaching traffic at least one-half of the road unless conditions or directions indicate otherwise.

2. **Signal Your Intentions** — "properly and adequately." You must give clear warning signals that are standard, appropriate to your intentions, and timed to give other drivers reasonable warning.

3. **Pass on the Left.** When overtaking and passing other vehicles, pass to the left and remain on the left until safely clear of the overtaken vehicle.

4. **Pass on the Right ONLY When ...** You may pass on the right when the vehicle you are passing has signaled and is making a left turn. You may also pass on the right if you are on a street or highway designed for two or more lanes of traffic in both directions or on a one-way street with at least two lanes. You may *NOT* pass on the right if you must drive off the pavement or the main portion of the roadway to get around another vehicle.

5. **Change Lanes Sparingly and Cautiously.** When changing lanes to pass another vehicle and return to your lane — or to position yourself for a turn or road exit — keep movement from one lane to another to the minimum. If you must change lanes, signal your intentions; then ensure that such movement can be made safely and does not interfere with the movement of traffic in other lanes.

6. **Turn the "Correct" Way** — To turn right at an intersection, approach the turn at the extreme right of the traveled way and make the turn itself as close to the right as practicable. To turn left, approach the turn to the right

of, and close to, the centerline, leaving the intersection to the right of the centerline of the entered road. A turn to reverse the direction of a vehicle (u-turn, where legal) should not be made unless a vehicle approaching from either direction can see the movement from a distance of 500 feet.

7. **Yield the Right of Way**. Observe the rules of right-of-way with judgment and courtesy. The safe driver gives the right-of-way rather than taking it.

8. **Observe Speed Limits**. Highway speeds to be observed under normal conditions vary somewhat from state to state. These speeds are generally posted on regulatory signs with warnings where reduction in speed is directed. At no time should vehicles be operated in excess of posted limits. Driver judgment should be consciously developed to determine speeds suitable to other conditions.

9. **Assess Your Moves — *Before* You Make Them**. Do *not* start, stop, or turn a vehicle from its course on the highway without ensuring that making such a change is reasonably safe. You must know how to judge the effect of YOUR vehicle's movement upon *another* vehicle's speed or direction.

> **Safe driving requires *constant* adjustment to changing driving conditions.**

WHAT THIS BOOK IS ABOUT

Although the rules of the road and the roads and vehicles themselves have changed over the years, remarkably much has remained the same. Vehicles now — as then — still have the same basic controls for accelerating (gas pedal), steering (steering wheel), and braking (brakes). And the physical principles that create forces on a vehicle as you maneuver it using these controls — friction, momentum, G-forces, centrifugal force — have the same effect now as they did then.

What we're getting at here is that **a "good driver" — a safe driver — is determined by qualities (knowledge and skills) of the driver him/herself.**

> **A "good" driver — a safe driver — knows and practices good, safe driving techniques — *regardless* of the vehicle he's driving, the road she's on, or the environment he's in.**

The book you hold in your hands, *Driving Techniques for the Professional and Non-Professional, 3rd Edition,* shows you how to develop all the knowledge and skills you need to become a "good" driver — a safe driver.

Part I, DRIVING IS A STATE OF MIND — AND BODY — AND VEHICLE.

This Part begins with **a discussion of the driver him/herself.** We explore, for example, the driver's physical and mental state; effects of fatigue; vision and sense of space (two key factors that underlie your ability to interpret and negotiate safely in the driving environment); and reaction time and sense of timing.

Then we look at the vehicle itself, focusing on features that directly affect driving safety and that a driver should know how to use properly and to maintain — the windshield, windshield wipers, mirrors, seat belts and child safety seats, air bags, and tires. These are all designed to help you maintain control of your vehicle, to help you drive safely, and to help you avoid serious injury if you are in a collision.

We then consider **some general maintenance rules for your vehicle** — what to check or have checked, and how often. We even include a convenient Ten Minute Checklist that covers 17 items to check, and when to check them.

This Part concludes with a look at **what should be inside every safe driver's glove compartment and trunk,** along with some cautions and warnings. You may never have cause to use some of the items — but if you ever have an emergency on the road, you'll be more than glad you have them.

Part II, THE SCIENCE AND TECHNIQUES OF EVERYDAY DRIVING

This Part is the meat of *Driving Techniques, 3rd Edition.* Most drivers never think of car control until an emergency occurs. When the emergency does occur, it's often too late to think about it. To control a car as efficiently and effectively as possible, you must understand some of the science — *as well as* the techniques — of driving.

So, this Part looks in detail at **the control maneuvers you can make with a car — accelerating, steering, braking.** It covers the basic science behind these maneuvers and discusses specific techniques you can use to maintain maximum control of your vehicle.

It also points out — perhaps more importantly — **what can happen if you *lose* control by not accelerating, steering, or braking *properly*** — and *WHY*. And it tells you **how to *regain* control** if you've lost it.

We'll look closely at major topics such as: vehicle dynamics; maintaining traction (tire-to-road grip and weight transfer); losing and regaining traction when the traction/weight transfer equation goes out of balance (how to handle braking skids, power skids, cornering skids); steering at speed and G-forces (how speed and tire adhesion enter into the steering control equation); techniques for safe cornering at speed; speed and stopping distances (time-distance relationship in stopping and turning); safe following distances; braking control (how a car stops; non-ABS and ABS techniques); proper turning techniques (turning left, turning right, backing up, and turning around); and passing and being passed. (when to pass, when NOT to pass, how to pass, and how to yield the right of way.)

Part III, ACCIDENTS

Part III, considers what can happen if either you, or the drivers around you on the road, *don't* maintain control — or you, or they, can't *regain* it.

We begin with a look at **current accident statistics to see the who, what, when, and how of accidents.** Then we explore **what causes accidents** (driver, environment, vehicle). Then we consider **typical accident scenarios and tell you how to avoid or deal with them.** And since you'll likely encounter not only vehicles, but pedestrians and bicyclists on the road as well, we give you tips on **how to safely "share the road."**

And finally we offer a Q&A "Crash Course" that provides some suggestions on **how you can help if you come upon or are involved in an accident yourself.**

Part IV, DRIVING IN SPECIAL SITUATIONS

Part IV looks at strategies and techniques for driving in situations that pose special hazards — **driving in foul weather of all types, driving at night, roadside breakdowns, road rage, and driving alone.**

Part V, RESOURCES

Part V provides list of **websites** where you can find the most up-to-date information on driving-related matters.

So, how can you become a "good driver" — a safe driver? *READ ON!*

PART I

Driving is a State of Mind— and Body — and Vehicle

In following chapters we look at the driver him/herself — physical and mental state, vision and sense of space, reaction time and sense of timing.

Then we look at the vehicle itself, focusing on the components that directly affect driving safety and that a driver should know how to use properly and to maintain — the windshield, wipers, mirrors, seat belts and child safety seats, air bags, and tires.

We then consider some general maintenance rules for your vehicle — what to check or have checked, and how often. We even include a convenient *Ten-Minute Checklist* that covers 17 items to check, and when to check them.

The Part concludes with a look at what should be inside every safe driver's glove compartment and trunk. You may never have cause to use some of the items — but if you ever have an emergency on the road, you'll be more than glad you have them.

Chapter 1

The Mind/Body Driving Connection

To drive in a safe and secure manner, you must be in good physical and mental condition. This is the very foundation of safe driving. If your driving ability is impaired by illness or injury, or by fatigue or the effect of medications — to say nothing of alcohol or illegal drugs — you should seriously consider *not* driving a vehicle.

How important is physical condition to safe driving? Consider this scenario:

> You have developed **a shoulder injury.** Thanks to your sore shoulder, it now takes you just a little longer to move the steering wheel — say, about one second longer.
>
> You are driving along at 40 mph when suddenly someone ahead of you runs a stop sign. Since you are traveling at 40 mph, you are also traveling at the rate of 58.8 feet per second. And, since it now takes you a second longer to react at the wheel, **you also need an *additional* 60 feet (more or less) to get out of the way.**

Those 60 feet could mean the difference between a wild story to tell at the office, or spending years recovering from injury — or worse.

And don't drive while you are emotionally unstable. Never let your emotions get hold of you while driving. Driving while emotionally upset, especially while unusually angry or sad, can reduce your ability to recognize danger and avoid it.

> **The solution to avoiding possible catastrophe is simple: if *anything* makes you feel like you can't drive, don't. If there is any way you can avoid it, avoid it.**

Physical and Mental Fatigue

A driver can be in excellent condition — and have the eyes of an eagle. But a driver, like all other mammals, has a central nervous system, and can get tired. Most drivers, however, often don't think that their fatigue at any given time is a serious impediment to their driving ability — until the fatigue becomes so serious that they are in real danger.

Physical fatigue can be caused by things you did *before* you even got into your vehicle. Driving into work after an all-night party may be a memorable experience, but if your condition is such that you have a hard time finding the door handle of the vehicle, you can wind up with an experience you'd rather forget. Sometimes just the realities of day-to-day living — such as an all-night session with a sick child or other personal emergencies — make it impossible to drive bright-eyed and bushy-tailed.

Mental fatigue can cause the same problems as physical fatigue. Worries over personal problems, irritation with someone on or off the job who just gave you a hard time — are some of the things that can cause mental fatigue. And you often don't get an opportunity to take a moment to unwind after a stressful day.

> **Driving tired or hung over can literally be fatal. You don't have to lead a life of sainthood, but your state of fatigue should never be *self-induced*.**

You can resist the effects of fatigue by simply being aware of them, knowing they exist, and being alert to the first warning signs.

The symptoms of fatigue are obvious. After all, everyone has had trouble keeping his or her eyes open at one time or another time. **However, the *early* signs of fatigue are NOT so obvious.** All of us have had the following experience:

> We drive a car down a route we travel every day. Nothing noteworthy happens on the drive, and at some point on the route — at an intersection, a bridge, wherever — we suddenly realize that we don't really recall the drive to that spot. It is as if we suddenly materialized at that intersection or bridge. *This is a strong warning that you are fatigued.*

And, if your eyelids are heavy and your eyes are burning, you're *definitely* fatigued!

And Just What Kinds of Problems Does Driving While Fatigued Create?

- **When driving at night, you may have a hard time concentrating on your driving.** This is no great revelation. When you are tired, you have a hard time concentrating on *anything* you do.

- **When fatigued, you tend to take more risks.** You may do things while fatigued you would *never* think of doing when well rested. Fatigue dulls your mind.

- **When you're tired, you may have a tough time keeping your car in the proper lane.** You may weave side to side and appear drunk, even though you're not. You're just very, very tired. But the results are the same. It's a dangerous, accident-producing situation.

- **When you're fatigued, you often speed up and slow down erratically.** If you often find yourself doing that, be aware of it. *You're fatigued.*

- **If you're fatigued and you ignore these early warning signals and continue to drive — you develop "tunnel vision."** Your vision deteriorates. It gradually becomes very difficult to see. Your attention focuses forward. You will begin to miss signals or signs in the peripheral vision area. This accounts, in part, for many of the accidents that occur near the end of a long day at work.

The surest way to recover from fatigue is to stop and rest or take a short nap.

The most successful driving is performed when the driver rests 20-30 minutes for every one-and-a-half to two hours of driving.

The time-honored cure of drinking coffee to stay awake is only a stopgap, temporary measure. Sure, the caffeine can bring you up fast, but as the kidneys eliminate it from the body, it will also bring you down fast.

Even a brief stop and just a leg-stretching short walk can be valuable in fighting fatigue.

Certain groups of people are at a higher risk of suffering from driver fatigue than others.

Some of the candidates may surprise you. Do you fit into one or more of these groups?

- Professional and over-the-road drivers
- Night-shift workers
- Law enforcement workers
- People who work shifts in excess of 12 hours
- Senior Citizens
- Smokers
- People with sleeping disorders

Here are some web sites that discuss the problems of fatigue.
http://www.nhtsa.dot.gov/people/perform/human/Drowsy.html
http://www.trafficsafety.org/

The Way You Sit in a Car Can Help You Remain Alert

There is no single clear-cut fool-proof way to beat fatigue — but seating position is often critical.

Many people blame car seats for an uncomfortable ride. Most of the time the seats aren't to blame — it's the way you sit in them. Sitting erect allows you to stay alert longer. Shoulder and arm positions are also important.

- **When you get into your vehicle, place your hand at the top of the steering wheel.** *Your shoulder should be in contact with the seat back.* If

Figure 1-1. Drive with Two Hands on the Steering Wheel in Proper Position — Photo © Jim Spencer/SeaNotes

your shoulder rises off the seat back, you'll find that when you execute an emergency maneuver, you'll be lifted right off your seat. Instead of using the steering wheel to control the car, you'll be using it to hold yourself in place.

- **Consider the steering wheel as a clock** — with the top as 12 o'clock and the bottom, six. Ideally, your hands should be at the three- and nine-o'clock positions. Both hands should remain on the wheel unless it is necessary to operate another control in the car with either hand.

- **As you sit comfortably, look at your arms.** If they are bent at the elbow more than 90 degrees, the result will be poor circulation and very tired arms in a short time.

- **One of the most common errors is caused by sitting too close to the steering wheel.** This often indicates a lack of confidence on the part of the driver, or poor eyesight, or both.

- **The opposite extreme, getting too relaxed behind the wheel, can also be a major problem.** A driver with the window rolled down, elbow propped up on the sill, and driving with one hand is probably just a little *too* relaxed and over-confident.

"Avoid Driving While Taking This Product"

All drugs — prescription, over-the-counter, and illegal — have the potential to suppress your brain's ability to process information. And the amount of information processing needed to control a vehicle can become more than an impaired brain can handle.

The warning "*Avoid driving while taking this medication*" appears on the back of many over-the-counter medications and on many prescription bottles. The makers of these medications are trying to tell you something. Even something as mild as a hay fever pill can seriously impair your ability to control a vehicle.

> **Read the label before you take *any* medication and then drive.**

If you're taking prescription medication, ask your doctor about the effects it may have on your driving. If it can have any negative effects, do whatever you can to avoid driving while on the medication.

Driving While under the Influence . . .

All tests examining **the role of alcohol in driving impairment** have indicated the same thing: alcohol reduces the capacity of the mind to process information from both the road and the overall-driving environment.

Similar tests performed using marijuana showed different results. Although reaction times were slowed by marijuana, they were not slowed as much as when test subjects were given alcohol. The conclusion would seem to be that marijuana is less dangerous than alcohol when it comes to driving. Nevertheless, it is still a dangerous, foolhardy, and illegal thing to do.

What happens when **driving under the influence of marijuana** is what has been termed a "perceptual failure" — you simply do not see things in time to react to the them. Put more bluntly, you're so stoned, you don't recognize you're in trouble until it is too late to do anything about it. There is very little good research data on marijuana and driving.

Chapter 2

Your Vision and Sense of Space

When driving, the most important aspect of your physical well-being is the quality of your eyesight. Every action you take behind the wheel is based on eye-hand and/or eye-foot co-ordination. Although you use *all* your senses when driving, over 90 percent of the information you need to control a vehicle comes from what you *see*.

And, equally important, you need to develop your sense of *space* while behind the wheel — where your vehicle is in relation to everything around you. You have to develop a *questioning attitude* that heightens your awareness of both what you can and *cannot* see.

- **You can't avoid an accident if you can't see it coming.**

- **You can't leave yourself an escape route for every maneuver you make** if you aren't aware of the space around you.

- **And you could potentially *cause* an accident yourself** if you cannot see the road and surroundings well.

PROTECTING YOUR VISION

Even if your eyesight is healthy — with or without corrective lenses — **hazards such as glare and the low light conditions of night** can make seeing difficult for anyone.

Even some features of **a car's design** can hinder your visibility while behind the wheel.

> **A safe driver knows how to protect his vision in all situations.**

Seeing at Night

The human eye works far better in daylight than in reduced light conditions. Plainly said, it's hard to see at night.

- Your **peripheral vision is decreased.**

- Your normally wide **field of vision is narrowed** to the field of view illuminated by your headlights, the headlights of other vehicles, and fixed road lights.

- When viewed **at night, most objects exhibit relatively low contrast,** which makes their detection, especially against certain backgrounds, extremely difficult.

- **Colors fade at night.**

- And **your eyes simply need time to adjust to low light conditions** before your night vision kicks in — and **the older you get,** the longer this adaptation process takes place.

Night vision

Dusk and dawn are the two most difficult times of the day for good vision. In the changing light of dawn and dusk, the eye is caught in the middle. At dusk, as the light fades and evening comes on, your eyes gradually adapt to the light and you are given the gift of night vision. But, until that happens, there will be a period of time when you cannot see very well.

At night, if you leave your well-lit house or office and go out and jump into your car and start off, it's the same as when you walk into a movie house after the picture has already started. There you are in a darkened theater, probably juggling an armload of popcorn and soda, trying to find a seat you simply cannot see. You blunder into a seat, stepping on a few toes on the way, and after a few minutes, you notice how much more light the theater has. Your eyes have had the time they need to adapt to the new lighting situation.

So, in those first minutes after you jump into your car, **you can blunder just as badly behind the wheel** as you can in a darkened movie theater — and that's one of the reasons that each and every day people run cars into each another in every imaginable way.

So when you get into a car at night, give your eyes a chance to adjust to the changes in light conditions *before* you head out on the road.

Effects of prolonged daylight exposure on night vision

Prolonged exposure to glare from sunlight during the day (or, similarly, from headlights at night) **can temporarily ruin your night vision,** and can also lead to eye strain and drowsiness.

To alleviate the effects of such exposure, wear good sunglasses on bright days and take them off as soon as the sun goes down. Also, rest a while before driving at night after a long session of steady daytime driving.

Protecting and Enhancing Your Driving Vision — Day and Night

Eye "protection" against the affects of glare and low-light conditions is important for driving whether or not you normally wear corrective lenses. And, as we'll see, there are some specifications for lenses that make both sunglasses and regular glasses better for driving than others. But regardless of the lens type, *all* eyewear should provide sufficient lens coverage for peripheral vision, non-obstructive frames and temple pieces, and lightweight, comfortable ear and nose pieces.

Sunglasses

Because the glare of sunlight on bright days can be blinding — and too much exposure to sunlight can affect your night vision — you should always wear sunglasses when driving during daylight hours.

> **Make sure you wear good-quality sunglasses. Buy them with consideration toward how well they'll treat your eyes — and not toward how good they look on you!**

Antireflective coating (AR)

If you wear eyeglasses and want to drive at peak efficiency day or night, wear glasses with an antireflection (AR) coating on the lenses.

The AR coating does much the same thing as similar coatings on binocular and camera lenses — it increases the lenses' efficiency by allowing them to transmit more light. At least 8 percent of the light is absorbed within a clear glass lens, but the same lens with an AR coating transmits 99 percent of the light.

Tints

- **Gray lenses worn during the day provide the right amount of light while properly preparing your eyes for the coming darkness.** After wearing gray lenses all day, your eyes will make the transition to reduced light levels much more readily, and what you see will be a much more accurate picture of what's really happening after dark.

- **Yellow lenses are recommended for night use** because the eye is most sensitive to the yellow portion of the spectrum, and because they effectively increase the apparent viewing brilliance and alleviate 20 percent of usual night-driving fatigue.

- **Yellow lenses also help on cloudy days,** but the effect is usually too brilliant for sunny weather.

- **Adding a yellow tint (for cosmetic purposes)** will not reduce the light transmission characteristics of the lenses below 92 percent as long as the lenses are AR coated.

Car Design and Visibility

You can do your part to protect your vision against the glary hazards of day and night driving, but **some features of a car's design** — while providing comfort in one way or another — **can actually make visibility difficult at night.** And there's not much you can do about it. But you should be aware of such features and understand how they can affect your ability to see at night.

- **Tinted glass,** which helps keep the interior temperature low during sunny days, also cuts visibility considerably in the dark of night.

- **Greenish or bluish tint of instrument panel lights** is bad for night vision. These colors are at the end of the spectrum to which the eye is *least* sensitive in low light.

- Many cars, however, come equipped with **red instrument lighting**, a practice that's been common for quite some time in the aircraft industry.

  Red light does not interfere with vision outside of the car, and it makes the instruments much clearer to read. Red panel lighting eliminates the endless squinting down at the panel and the need for the eyes to continually readjust from glances at the instruments, or gazes at the road. This does much to reduce overall eye fatigue and makes long night drives more comfortable.

> See Ch. 27, *Driving Safely at Night* for additional tips on how to prepare for and combat the hazards of low-light conditions on the road.

The Myth of "Tired" Eyes

At one time or another all of us have complained of **tired eyes**. But the eyes *themselves* do not tire. The nerves, brain, and body fatigue. The heavy eyelids and burning sensation that most people associate with tired eyes are really the physical reactions of a **tired body.**

If your eyes become "tired" while you're driving, heed the warnings of oncoming fatigue and take the necessary precautions. (See the discussion on Physical and Mental Fatigue, p. 12.) *Don't drive tired!*

SELECTIVE VISION AND YOUR SENSE OF SPACE

A great deal of the success of the various safe driving and emergency maneuvers depends on the driver's alertness and powers of observation. You must know what is going on *at all times* around your vehicle, and you must *anticipate* what can and might happen. You need *space* all around your vehicle, because when things go wrong, space gives you time to think and act. And to have space *available* for when something goes wrong, you need to *manage* space.

Looking Near, Looking Far

Not looking properly is a major cause of accidents. Don't just base your driving performance on what you can see directly in front of you. **All drivers look ahead, but many do not look *far enough* ahead.** Stopping or changing lanes can take a lot of distance, so you must know what the traffic is doing on all sides of you. You must look far enough ahead to be sure you have room to move — or stop — safely.

> **Perhaps the most important thing to remember is that you should be able to *stop* your car within the distance you can *SEE*. You'll learn the real importance of this in Ch. 17, *Speed and Safe Stopping Distances*.)**

- **Most good drivers look 12 to 15 seconds ahead.** That means looking ahead the distance you will *travel* in 12 to 15 seconds.

- **At lower speeds**, that is about **one block;** at **highway speeds**, about **a quarter of a mile.**

- **If you do *not look* that far ahead,** you may have to stop too quickly or change lanes quickly.

Looking 12 to 15 seconds ahead does not mean not paying attention to *closer* things. **Good drivers shift their attention back and forth, near and far.**

- Look for **what could be lurking** around **corners,** on the other side of **hills,** and moving through **intersections**.

- Look for **vehicles** coming onto the highway, into your lane, or turning.

- Watch for **brake lights** from **slow moving vehicles.**

- Look for **hills, curves,** or anything **for which you must slow down or change lanes.**

- **Pay attention to traffic signals and signs.** If a light has been green for a long time, it will probably change before you get there. Start slowing down and be ready to stop. Traffic signs may alert you to road conditions where you may have to change speed.

> By seeing these things far enough ahead, you can change your speed or change lanes if necessary to avoid a problem.

Always Leave Yourself an "Out"

One of the basic points about avoiding accidents is easy to understand and very fundamental to safe driving: **Leave yourself an out — an escape route for every move you make.**

To do this, you have to **be aware of *what's going on around you* all the time.** Your best tools for doing this are your mirrors, both rearview and sideview. (Too many of us only use our rearview mirrors when we want to pull out into traffic.)

- **Use all your mirrors in order to see the big picture.** You need accurate information about what's going on on your right, left, and rear.

In an emergency situation, such as a collision right in front of you, you need all the information you can get about what's happening around you, and you need it fast. Mirrors are your best way of getting this information. *(See Ch. 4, Windshields and Mirrors* for tips on how to properly adjust and use your vehicle's mirrors.)

Sense of Space in Traffic Situations

It's hard to avoid traffic. *All* of us have to drive in traffic. It's impossible to avoid, so we learn to live with it. It's a fact of life.

In **heavy, stop-and-go traffic,** it's *vital* to pay attention to what's going on around you. That can be tough because, from minute to minute, it may not seem like much *is* happening, especially if the traffic isn't moving very fast.

- Keep your eyes and *mind* **focused on the tasks in front of you.**

- **Maintain a safe distance** from the car in front of you.

- Be watchful for **cars pulling out of parking spots**. Many do so without looking where they are heading.

- Watch out for **the distracted person** — the one with the map or the one trying to read the directions he's been given to the local Moose hall, trying to spot landmarks and otherwise relate his directions to the world around him — all the while not looking where he's going at all.

And there's another kind of traffic — one that's even more deadly — **high-speed traffic.** This is traffic bunched together and moving at high speed. Cars are being driven very fast, very close to one another. There's not much you can do about this. **Try to give all the vehicles around you as much space as you can.**

Chapter 3

Your Reaction Time/Sense of Timing

What Is Reaction Time?

Many factors can affect your reaction time, but before we talk about them, let's find out just what reaction time is.

Reaction time is the sum of the time needed for:

1. **The brain to receive information from the senses.** The senses we're referring to also include sensations of motion and related "seat of the pants" sensations.

2. **Making decisions on what to do next.** Many times, this is a reflexive reaction that carries a potential for danger with it, such as immediately smashing down on the brake pedal when we feel the car begin to skid.

3. **Transmission of the messages from the brain to the muscles needed to react and move the controls.**

4. **The muscles to respond**.

> **The most critical portion of the reaction process is Step #2. After the senses detect the danger, a decision has to be made about what to do with the received information.**

The challenges and dangers faced by racing drivers present a good example of this process

Many racing drivers are surprisingly "old." Their reflexes may not be quite what they were when they were younger, but the *decisions* they make in the course of a race are the right ones.

These decisions are based on their years of experience behind the wheel. Knowledge gained through experience often becomes *intuitive*, so that it becomes part of our reflex reaction. Experienced pilots often gain this sort of reflexive knowledge.

A Hypothetical Example of Reaction Time/Sense of Timing

As an example, let's set up a hypothetical situation with two drivers, one young, and the other much older. Both are driving vehicles equipped with standard (non-ABS) brakes. (See Figure 3-1, p. 31.)

- They are both driving toward the same intersection from opposite directions.

- Ahead of them, a truck runs a stop sign and illegally enters the intersection so as to block the path of both drivers' cars.

- **The younger driver gets his foot on the brake before the older driver,** but smashes the pedal to the floor and locks up both front wheels, enters an uncontrollable skid, and crashes into the truck.

- **The older driver takes more time to react,** but once he does, he brakes carefully, applies the proper amount of brake force and steering control and avoids the collision.

- **The younger driver won the race to the brake pedal, but lost the battle with the truck.**

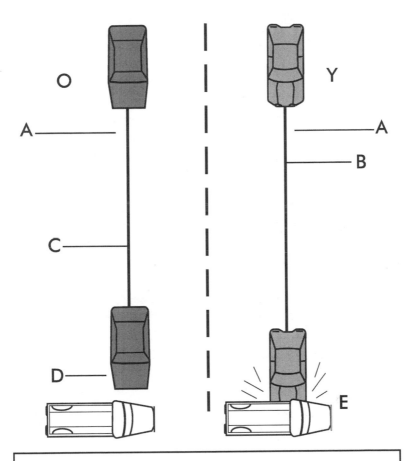

Figure 3-1. Reflexes vs Decision Making.

Car "Y" driven by young man.

Car "O" driven by older gentleman.

At point A both see emergency.

Car "Y" reaction time to get his foot to the brake is 0.5 sec., which will use up 45 feet. Point B.

Car "O" reaction time to the brake is 1 sec., which will use up 90 feet. Point C.

Car "Y" driver has slammed on the brake, locking up both wheels. The car enters an uncontrollable skid, lasting 1.5 seconds or 135 feet. Car "O" takes 0.5 sec. to make a decision; he travels 45 feet.

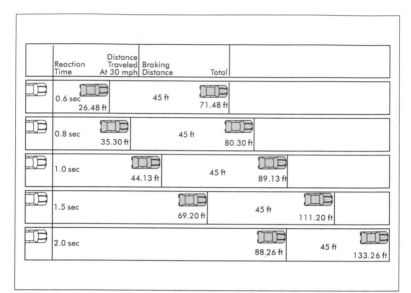

Reaction Time	Distance Traveled At 30 mph	Braking Distance	Total	
0.6 sec	26.48 ft	45 ft	71.48 ft	
0.8 sec	35.30 ft	45 ft	80.30 ft	
1.0 sec	44.13 ft	45 ft	89.13 ft	
1.5 sec	69.20 ft	45 ft	111.20 ft	
2.0 sec	88.26 ft	45 ft	133.26 ft	

Figure 3-2. Reaction Time Diagram. The effects of various reaction times on total stopping distances.

> **Without intuitive experience, the quickest decision can easily be the *wrong* decision.**

Many Factors Other Than Age Affect Reaction Time

Reaction times can vary a great deal between people of the same age group.

Reaction times can vary according to the time of day — as much as four-tenths of a second in the morning to as much as a full second when a driver is fatigued at day's end. Four-tenths of a second may not sound like much, but at 60 mph a car travels 35 ft. in that amount of time. That could make a life and death difference in an accident situation. (See Figure 3-2, p. 32.)

Reaction times among tired or ill drivers can be as long as two full seconds. Again, at 60 mph, that means a driver will cover 123 ft. before reacting to a threat.

> **The standard reaction time for a healthy person is .75 sec.**

Decision Making Behind the Wheel

After an accident, some people might ask, *Why did the driver just drive into the other car when there were so many other options open to him?*

The answer could simply be that the driver could not *reach* a decision before it was too late. **The time required by the brain for a simple decision depends on how complex that decision is.**

- **A simple decision,** such as a reflex action, can be reached in **three-tenths of a second.**

- **If the problem faced by the brain is sufficiently complex** to require some thought, that decision can take as long as **five-tenths to two full seconds**, depending on the available options and the capabilities of the individual.

Over-Dependence on Reaction Time

The most important lesson to be learned about reaction time is that we know *not* to depend on it to get us out of trouble. The classic example of over-dependence on reaction time is encountered in the tailgater.

The Tailgater — The classic example of over-dependence on reaction time

We have all been plagued by this kind of driver — the one that drives too fast and so close you can practically count the fillings in his teeth in the rear-view mirror.

An emergency can easily and quickly develop with no way for someone following you so closely to have adequate time and enough room to react. The tailgater is going to smash into you if you have to stop quickly, that's for sure.

If you were to pull that tailgater over and ask him why he follows you so closely, you might encounter someone who honestly doesn't know what you're talking about, someone that really doesn't consider what he's doing as something dangerous, or, more disturbingly, someone who thinks he is Superman — the super-driver that can react to anything, handle any driving emergency. Both attitudes are idiotic.

Training *Can* Improve Reaction Time

While it cannot make muscles move faster, training can cut the time required in reaching a decision.

Through training, a driver can experience situations simulating driving emergencies. This:

- Helps **build the decision-making process.**

- Encourages the driver to focus attention on **the proper course of action in a given emergency situation.**

- Helps drivers stay aware of **their own limitations and that of their vehicles.**

IN THE NEXT SEVERAL CHAPTERS, we move on to examine the features of the car itself that — if used and maintained properly — are designed to help you maintain control of your vehicle, to help you drive safely, and to help you avoid serious injury if you are in a collision.

Chapter 4

The Windshield and Mirrors:

Your "Windows" to the Road

Vision is a complex sense, affected by a number of variables, many of which you have no control over. Your vision inside the car is not only affected by your own physical limitations, but by factors such as tinted windshields and convex rearview or sideview mirrors that can distort the image you see in the mirror.

THE WINDSHIELD

Perhaps the most important window you look through in your car is the windshield.

Windshield Visibility

Just how much visibility do you have when looking through a windshield? A non-tinted windshield permits 89 percent of the perpendicular light to pass through. Since almost no modern vehicles have perpendicular windshields (the exceptions being Jeeps and other utility vehicles), the real-world windshield value in this area is more like 82 to 84 percent of the light.

What does the National Highway Traffic Safety Administration (NHTSA) have to say about this? Their rule is that the windshield needs to pass only 70 percent of the light to meet safety standards — and that is as measured through a perpendicular windshield.

*The result is that most windshields on commercially available cars today permit about **62 percent of 65 percent** of the light to come through.*

Clear away the fog

NEVER drive with a fogged windshield (or side mirrors). This sounds pretty elementary, I know. Yet we've all seen people driving down the road with a windshield nearly completely fogged. Usually they've managed to clear a little peephole in the windshield, but their side and rear windows are completely fogged or covered with snow. Their cars look like little tanks, with the drivers peering through tiny slits. You cannot *afford* to indulge in such foolishness.

Clear away the grime — inside and out

It's amazing just how much grime and dust can accumulate on the outside and *inside* of a windshield, the windows, and on the mirrors.

Most drivers, if they clean their windshields at all, concentrate on the *outside*. But it's just as important to keep the *inside* clean as well. Clear visibility is important in driving *at all times,* but it takes on a whole new meaning when you're driving at night and in foul weather. (See Chs. 26, *Foul Weather Driving*, and 27, *Driving Safely at Night*.)

If you smoke in your vehicle, the accumulation of grime is even worse! **If you smoke or drive with someone who does,** clean the inside of the windshield *every other day*. It's amazing how fast smoke residue builds up on the inside of a car's windshield.

Do not drive **until you have cleared *all* windows and mirrors — *INSIDE* and *OUT*.**

REMEMBER: Clear vision is the foundation of safe driving.

Windshield Wipers

Perhaps the most important safety feature of all is right in front of your eyes — yet you tend not to see them or pay much attention to them until they don't work: your inexpensive windshield wipers.

Although many drivers take their wipers for granted, when they're needed, they're needed _now_. It doesn't take long for wiper blades to deteriorate, and if they're not in good working condition when you click on the switch, you can be left virtually blind for crucial moments of driving time. To avoid an accident, you need to see it developing; therefore, the benefits of a clean windshield are obvious — you can see better.

Figure 4-1. Keep Your Windshield Clean.
Dan Raber of Key Largo, Florida, frequently cleans pollen and
mosquitoes from his windshield.
Photo ©Jim Spencer/SeaNotes

A clean windshield is vital for driving, whether in day or night. Streaks and smears on windshields can produce extremely disorienting kaleidoscopic effects when lights shine on them at night. Make sure your windshield washers work, that your windshield wiper blades are clean and not old and worn out, and that the windshield wiper fluid container is kept filled.

How do you make wipers work better and last longer? You can add years to the life of your wiper blades—and get a clearer windshield in the bargain—just by taking a few extra seconds to "wipe your wipers."

> "We recommend cleaning your windshield wipers regularly with a clean cloth soaked in windshield washer fluid," says Dick Hazell, Reliability Engineer for Delco Chassis (which designs and manufactures wiper systems and components for General Motors). "We suggest cleaning them every second or third time you wash your car — more often if you notice your wipers streaking."

Wiping your wiper blades with windshield washer fluid removes dirt, oil, bird droppings, and oxidized rubber from the edges and keeps the cleaning edge clean. The safety benefits are obvious: you'll see better in rain and sleet — especially at night — with streak-free wipers.

In dry weather, you should operate the wipers about once a week for a minute or so to prevent heat set. Be sure to keep the windshield well-lubricated with washer fluid or spray from a hose while the wipers are operating — *don't run them on dry glass*. While you're at it, clean the windshield using a good ammonia-based glass cleaner. With care, a set of wiper blades should last for one or two years, depending on the operating environment.

In harsh winter conditions, ice and snow can wreak havoc with a wiper's ability to keep the windshield clear. That's where special-purpose winter blades come in. Anco's winter design covers the wiper assembly and all of the moving parts with a neoprene boot. This protects the arms from the elements and prevents snow and ice from packing into them. Trico offers a similar design for its Winterblade. In addition, the winter wiper's compound is softer to help maintain flexibility when the mercury dips, the profile is a

little larger to help plow snow off the windshield, and it's heavier to provide more strength in its clearing action.

> **(See Ch. 9, *Smart Car Care* for additional tips on keeping your wipers in their best possible condition.)**

REARVIEW AND SIDEVIEW MIRRORS

How many times have you been driving down the road and another driver moving in the same direction drives into your lane. Either the person obviously did not see you in her mirrors, or simply did not look before turning the steering wheel. Many times you blame the latter for the problem, but in reality the driver *did* look, but just did not see you. His/her mirrors where not adjusted properly.

All vehicles must have one to three mirrors — by law. But all vehicles *should* have three mirrors. There is no excuse at all for having cars with only two mirrors (a rearview and left-side mirror). Most people don't understand the importance of a right-side mirror.

- **Having no right-side mirror** assumes no one will ever pass you on the right, or that you will never have to move to the right.

- It is also necessary that **all the mirrors be adjustable from the _driver's_ position.** You should not have to reach across the car to adjust the right-side mirror.

How Important Are Mirrors?

Without them, the only way you know what's behind you or coming along side you would be to turn and look. It only takes a second or two to look and that may not seem like much, but at 50 mph a car is traveling at the rate of 75 feet per second. If you look over your shoulder for two seconds, you would cover 150 feet without the knowledge of what's going on in front of you. At 65 mph you would cover almost 200 feet.

You cannot afford to turn and look while driving on a highway or in slow city driving. Your attention _must_ focus on what's in front of you. Reaction time and braking time could all be gone in two seconds.

If you are about to pass another vehicle and use a convex side mirror, remember that it is not to be used as an accurate indication of where the other car is in relation to your vehicle — it just indicates that the other vehicle is _there._

You should be cognizant of what is in your mirrors every few seconds, because traffic changes — and so do your escape routes. Properly adjusted mirrors could give you the emergency time you need to avoid an accident.

Adjusting the Mirrors

1. **Start with the right-side mirror.** (See Figure 4-2, p. 41) Adjust it so it gives a clear view of traffic on your right (Zone 1). It must be adjusted so you can see a vehicle, or part of a vehicle, on the right until your peripheral vision picks up the vehicle on the right. Therefore, as the vehicle leaves your vision in Zone 2 (rearview mirror), it must appear in Zone 1 (the right-side

mirror). As the vehicle leaves Zones 1 and 2, it must appear in your peripheral vision.

2. **Now adjust the center mirror (rearview mirror)** (Zone 2). The center mirror will cover everything directly behind you, but it also covers the blind spot on your right that your right-side mirror fails to pick up. It must also cover part of the left side of the vehicle where you will also have a blind spot on the left-side mirror. The rearview mirror must be adjusted so that as a vehicle disappears from it's view, it will appear in one of the side mirrors (Zone 1 or Zone 3).

3. **Now adjust the left-side mirror.** Adjust it so you can see a vehicle coming up on your left side and keep it in view until your peripheral vision picks it up.

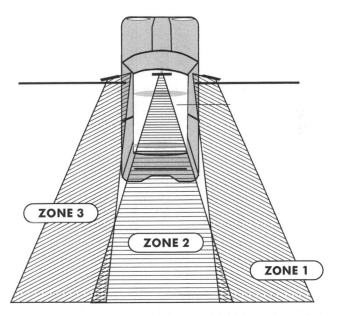

Figure 4-2. Mirror Zones. Rearview and sideview mirrors (left-side and right-side) must be adjusted properly to give you the maximum view of your driving environment. Checking that view every few seconds keeps you aware of changes in traffic, aware of possible escape routes should you need one, and gives you the emergency time you need to avoid an accident.

Why is it so important to know if a car is coming up behind you? When you have to make an evasive action, you need to know what's behind you and what may inhibit a move either left or right. Therefore, when the vehicle leaves the rearview mirror (Zone 2), it must appear in the left-side mirror (Zone 3). When it leaves the left-side mirror it must appear in the driver's peripheral vision.

"Blind Spots"[1]

Virtually all cars have "blind spots," spots where it's difficult to see cars close behind them to the left or right.

1. **To tell if you're driving in someone's blind spot,** just glance at his rearview mirror. If you can't see his face, assume he can't see you.

2. **Move forward or fall back so he can see you.**

3. **If you're behind a car at a *diagonal* angle,** you could be in its blind spot.

3. **There are probably blind spots in *your* car, too.** That's why it's always safer to *quickly* turn to visually check for other vehicles traveling in lanes next to yours before you pull over. [However, don't turn around so long that you compromise your ability to stop quickly should a situation develop in front of you.]

> **The Vampire Rule — Another place to check to see if you're in someone's blind spot is the outside mirror. If you can't see the driver's face, chances are he/she can't see you.**

---

[1] Copyright Shell Oil Company material written by Mike Carpenter, used with permission.

Chapter 5

Seat Belts and Child Safety Seats

SEAT BELTS

The facts are in on seat belts: THEY SAVE LIVES. Plain and simple. People have sometimes questioned the use of seat belts, expressing fears that belts could get in the way of fast exits from the car. But by *not* wearing a seat belt, you could experience a faster — and *deadly* — exit: right through the windshield or a flung-open door.

Even in a minor fender-bender you could be bounced around severely inside the car. And just *think* about what would happen in a **rollover.**

> **THERE IS NO EXCUSE FOR NOT WEARING A SEAT BELT!**

Why Do We Need Seat Belts?

It's amazing that even some driving *professionals* ask that question when the answer is so obvious. Sure, we all know the story of the guy who didn't wear a belt and was tossed free of the car in the accident when the car blew up and became an inferno. That guy must be the most popular man in the world because everybody knows him. Stop and think about this story. Can you imagine what it would be like to be thrown free or jump out of a car that was moving along at 40 mph? It could ruin your whole day. Along with your face, and most of what's attached to it.

Wearing a seat belt is merely a recognition of Sir Isaac Newton's Laws of Motion. Objects at rest tend to stay that way; likewise, moving objects tend to keep moving. A large, stationary object, such as a roadside telephone pole or tree, wants to stay that way. Your car, traveling towards that stationary object, wants to keep moving. When the stationary and the moving meet, something has to give. Generally, those "something's" are you and your car.

When your car hits the pole, it stops. Unfortunately, unless you are secured to the car by a seat belt, *you* don't stop moving. You travel forward to meet — and sometimes go through — the windshield. Seat belts are designed to keep this from happening.

Rollover crashes can be particularly injurious to vehicle occupants because of the unpredictable motion of the vehicle. In a rollover crash, unbelted occupants can be thrown against the interior of the vehicle and strike hard surfaces such as steering wheels, windows and other interior components. They also have a great risk of being ejected, which usually results in very serious injuries. Ejected occupants also can be struck by their own or other vehicles.

How to Wear a Seat Belt Properly

If your seat belt is uncomfortable, you're probably not wearing it properly.

A lot of people complain that seat belts are uncomfortable — and many people don't wear them for that reason. Try wearing a neck brace or spending a few weeks in traction. You'll *really* know what discomfort is.

- **Belts should be worn so there is none of the slack that allows the body to move forward before being stopped by the belt.** In a severe collision, a too-loose belt might produce bruises, but bruises are far better than having your face introduced to the windshield.

- **The lap portion of the belt should be comfortable but tight.**

- **The buckle should never be over your stomach**. It should be at your side, on the hip.

Most cars today have **inertia-reel seat belts** that allow passengers and drivers freedom of movement inside the car, while retaining the ability to lock in place when sudden tension, such as that encountered in a sudden stop or collision, takes place.

> **Where mandatory seat belt laws are in effect, automobile fatalities have gone down. That is not speculation. That is fact.**

If you're going to be a responsible, safe driver, you must take responsibility for the safety of your *passengers* as well as yourself. Make sure all adults wear their seat belts and that all children are secured in child safety seats.

CHILD SAFETY SEATS[1]

For Short Trips, Why Bother with a Child Safety Seat?

The greatest number of crashes occur on short trips at low speeds. Three-fourths of all crashes happen within 25 miles of home. And 40% of all fatal crashes take place on roads where the speed limit is 45 mph or less.

---

[1] Copyright Shell Oil Company material, used with permission.

> **THINK OF A CHILD SAFETY SEAT AS A
> *LIFE* PRESERVER.**

An Adult's Lap Is Pretty Safe, Right?

Wrong. **Grown-up arms are no substitute for a safety restraint.** In a 30-mph crash, a child is thrown forward with a force equal to 20 times his or her weight. Plus, **if the adult is not wearing a safety belt,** the child could get crushed between the adult and the windshield or dashboard.

When Are *Kids* Big Enough for a Regular Seat Belt?

In general, **when they're over 80 pounds and approximately eight years of age.** Too many children start using regular belts too soon. Your child has a proper fit when:

- **The lap belt stays low and snug across the hips** without riding up over the stomach.

- The **shoulder belt does not cross the face or front of the neck.**

There Are So Many Kinds of Safety Seats. Which One Is Best?

> **The best child safety seat is the one that fits the child, fits the vehicle, and can be installed and used correctly every time.**

There are **three basic types:**

1. **Rear-facing infant seats** are designed **for babies from birth until at least 20 pounds and one year of age.** Rear-facing infant car seats are small and

portable and fit newborns best. Don't confuse them with infant carriers.

2. **Convertible safety seats** "convert" from rear-facing to forward-facing **for toddlers between one and four years of age, who weigh between 20 and 40 pounds.** Convertible seats are used rear-facing for infants and forward-facing for toddlers.

3. **Booster seats** are used as **a transition to safety belts by older kids who have clearly outgrown their convertible seat but are not quite ready for the vehicle's belt system.** A booster seat raises the child so that the lap and shoulder belts fit properly. If your car only has lap belts, use a shield booster.

> **IN ALL CASES, check your owner's manual and car seat instructions to see if you need a "locking clip" to help secure the child's seat. It comes with all seats.**

Why Does an Infant Seat Have to Face the Rear?

Babies need the extra protection provided by the back of the safety seat, which absorbs and spreads the force of the crash. The infant's neck muscles are weak. If the baby faces forward, the head could snap forward in a crash, risking serious injury to the neck and spinal cord.

> **NEVER PUT A REAR-FACING INFANT SEAT IN THE FRONT WHEN THERE'S A PASSENGER AIR BAG.**
>
> **Air bags inflate at speeds up to 200 mph!**
>
> **A safety seat in the front puts the child too close to the bag when it's inflating and can cause serious injury or death.**

How Do I Make Sure the Child Safety Seat Is Working Properly?

Always read the instructions that come with a child safety seat (keeping them handy at all times), and read all sections in your vehicle owner's manual that discuss safety seat installation.

> **This is especially important because many child safety seats and vehicle belt systems are *not* compatible.**

Children are properly restrained *only* when:

1. **The child fits securely in the safety seat,** AND

2. **The safety seat itself fits securely in the vehicle seat.** If it doesn't, contact the safety seat manufacturer. Don't forget to mail in the registration card that comes with a new seat. Then the manufacture can let you know of any problems or recalls.

Where's the Safest Place for Kids in the Car?

The back seat is the safest place for a child of *any* age. And the safest place in the back seat is in the center — if you have center belts and an appropriate vehicle seat. **The most distance from impact usually means the most protection.** In the back, the child is farther away from the impact of a head-on collision, which can cause the most serious injuries. Just as important, the child is safely removed from the passenger air bag.

But I'm Not Comfortable with My Child in the Back. Shouldn't She Be Closer to Me?

No. The back seat is the safest. It may help to compare your child in the back to when your child is home sleeping. You probably don't feel the need to be right next to your baby all through the night or during a nap. A healthy baby properly secured in a safety seat should not need constant watching.

> **If a child in the back *does* need attention, don't try any one-hand-on-the wheel maneuvers. Just pull over.**

If an Older Child *Must* Be Seated in Front

If an older child must be seated in front, make sure he or she is correctly restrained for age and size — and **always slide the vehicle seat as far back as possible** — to put *maximum* distance between the child and an air bag.

> **See Ch. 6, *Air Bags: How They Work and Precautions to Take,* for a detailed discussion of the proper positioning of children in a car to protect them from potential air bag injury.**

> Box 5-1. **Child Safety Checklist**
>
> **Get in the habit of asking yourself some key questions about your child's safety *before* turning on the ignition:**
>
> ☑ Is my child riding in the back seat properly restrained?
>
> ☑ Is the safety seat facing the right way?
>
> ☑ Are belts and harness straps secured tightly?
>
> ☑ Is my older child wearing the seat belt correctly?

REDUCED SPEED 35

Chapter 6

Air Bags:

How They Work and Precautions to Take[1]

Standard driver-side and passenger-side air bags are designed to save lives and prevent injuries by cushioning vehicle occupants as they move forward in a moderate-to-severe front-end or near front-end crash. They keep the occupants' head, neck, and chest from hitting the steering wheel or dashboard.

> **Air bags inflate when the crash forces are about equivalent to striking a brick wall head-on at 10-15 miles per hour or a similar-sized vehicle head-on at 20-30 mph.**

Standard driver-side and passenger-side air bags are *not* designed to deploy in side, rear, or rollover crashes. (As we will discuss later, however, special side air bags are available for some vehicles.)

> **Since standard driver-side and passenger-side air bags provide *supplemental* protection only in frontal crashes, safety belts should always be used to provide maximum protection in rollovers and all crashes. (See Ch. 5, *Seat Belts and Child Safety Seats*.)**

---

[1] Material in this chapter was supplied by the National Highway Traffic Safety Administration.

**Figure 6-1 Front and Passenger-Side Air Bags —
Deployed.** Photo © Courtesy Mercedes-Benz USA, LLC

Check your owner's manual to see whether or not your vehicle is equipped with air bags, and whether or not you have a passenger-side air bag. Check for a warning label on the sun visor and/or the front of the right door frame. A passenger-side air bag is in a compartment in the dash board. The compartment *may* have a cover labeled SRS (Supplemental Restraint System) or SIR (Supplemental Inflation Restraint).

Since model year 1998, all new passenger cars have dual air bags (driver and passenger side). Starting in model year 1999, all new light trucks have dual air bags. Each vehicle is equipped with a unique air bag which will deploy with a different force.

HOW AIR BAGS WORK

Air Bag System Components

Most air bag systems consist of three main components:

- An **air bag module**
- One or more **crash sensors**

- A **diagnostic unit**

The **air bag module,** which contains an inflator and a vented, lightweight fabric air bag, sits in the hub of the steering wheel on the driver side ,and, if the vehicle is so equipped, in the instrument panel (dashboard) on the passenger side.

Crash sensor(s), on the front of the vehicle or in the passenger compartment, measure deceleration — the rate at which a vehicle slows down. When these sensors detect rapid decelerations that indicate a crash, they send a signal to the inflator that deploys the bag.

The **diagnostic unit** monitors the readiness of the air bag system whenever the vehicle ignition is turned on and the engine is running. A warning light on the dashboard will alert the driver if the air bag system needs service.

Once an air bag is deployed, it cannot be reused. Air bag system parts must be replaced by an authorized service dealer for the system to once again be operational.

Rapid Deployment

The entire deployment, inflation, and deflation cycle is over in less than one second.

- **The bag inflates within about 1/20th of a second after impact.**

- **At 1/5th of a second following impact, the air bag begins to deflate** and **deflates rapidly** as the gas escapes through vent holes or through the porous air bag fabric.

- **Initial deflation enhances the cushioning effect of the air bag** by maintaining approximately the same internal pressure as the occupant strikes into the bag.

- **Rapid deflation enables the driver to maintain control** if the vehicle is still moving after the crash, and prevents the driver and/or the right-front passenger from being trapped by the inflated air bag.

Dust

Dust particles present during the inflation cycle come from dry powder used to lubricate the tightly-packed air bag to ease rapid unfolding during deployment. Small amounts of particulate produced from combustion within the inflator also are released as gas is vented from the air bag. **These dust particles may produce minor throat and/or eye irritation.**

SIDE AND CURTAIN AIR BAGS

A number of auto manufacturers offer side-mounted and curtain-like side air bags which deploy from the roof and may span the entire side of the passenger compartment.

Figure 6-2. Side Air Bags - Deployed.
Photo © Courtesy Mercedes-Benz USA, LLC

Figure 6-3. Curtain Air Bags - Deployed.
Photo © Courtesy Mercedes-Benz USA, LLC

- **Side air bags** protect drivers and front-seat adult passengers in certain **side-impact collisions.** (A few manufacturers offer side air bags in the rear seat, too.)

  Side impact air bags can provide **significant safety benefits to *adults*;** however, as with ALL air bags (as we shall see), *children* seated in close proximity to a side air bag may be at risk of serious or fatal injury, especially if the child's head, neck, or chest is in close proximity to the air bag at the time of deployment.

  > **Because there are variations in the design and performance of side air bags, you should carefully read your owner's manual to see if it is safe for children to sit next to the side air bags.**

- **Curtain air bags** come down along the window to protect your head and neck. The curtain air bags work in conjunction with side air bags and can prevent both front and rear occupants from hitting their heads on the side windows or roof pillars in a severe side collision.

Plus, the air-filled cushion can block glass splinters or other objects that could cause injuries in a side impact or rollover.

- **Door-mounted air bags** break out of the armrest of the door just above the armrest. These protect your chest.

- **Seat-mounted systems** deploy from the side of the seat-back cushion closest to the door. Some inflate to the size of a small pillow, while others can inflate to the size of a large cushion. The smaller ones shield your chest, while the larger ones protect both your head and chest.

PRECAUTIONS TO TAKE

Whether a deploying air bag is an effective lifesaver or a danger *itself* depends on where and how occupants are seated and restrained in the vehicle.

The Risk Zone

- **The force of a deploying air bag is greatest in the first 2-3 inches** after the air bag bursts through its cover and begins to inflate. Those 2-3 inches are the "risk zone."

- **The force decreases as the air bag inflates further.**

- **Occupants who are very close to, or in contact with, the cover of a stored air bag** when the air bag begins to inflate **can be hit with enough force to suffer serious injury or death.**

- In contrast, **occupants who are properly restrained** and **who sit 10 inches away from the air bag cover** will contact the air bag only after it has completely or almost completely inflated. The air bag then will cushion and protect them from hitting hard surfaces in the vehicle and thus provide a significant safety benefit, particularly in moderate to serious crashes.

> **The big danger is contact with or close proximity to the air bag module at the *initial* instant of deployment.**

Air Bag Fatalities

On the driver side, fatally-injured drivers have been those who are believed to have sat close to their steering wheels either by habit or because they couldn't reach the steering wheel or gas and brake pedals if they sat farther back. Some had grown accustomed to sitting close to their steering wheel as matter of a preference.

On the passenger side, it has been primarily *children* who get too close to the air bag; however, confirmed adult deaths involving passenger-side air bags have also been caused by their proximity to the air bag when it deployed. The most common reason for the adults' proximity was failure to use seat belts.

Most passenger-side air bag fatalities have been infants and young children. Older children killed by frontal air bags were either unbelted or improperly belted and moved too close to the air bag during braking.

> **Some air bag fatalities have been attributed to the air bag's *design*. As a result, new air bag designs deploy first *radially* and *then* toward the occupant. Advanced air bags adjust deployment force or suppress deployment altogether.**

Protecting Yourself and Your Passengers from Potential Air Bag Injury

Children

> All new cars must have labels placed con-
> spicuously on the sun visors, dashboards, and
> child restraints to highlight the *dangers* of placing
> children in the front seat of vehicles with air bags.

- **Rear-facing infant car seats** place infants in great
  danger in the front seat because the child's head is too
  close to the dashboard where the air bag is stored.

> Infants in rear-facing car seats in vehicles
> with passenger-side air bags should **NEVER**
> be placed in the front seat. Period.

- **Older children in the front seat** get too close
  when they are allowed to ride completely unrestrained.
  During pre-crash braking, these unrestrained children
  slide forward and are up against or very near the
  dashboard when the air bag begins to deploy. Because
  of their proximity, the children can sustain fatal head or
  neck injuries from the deploying passenger air bag.

- Similarly, some **children who wear seat belts,
  but who are really too small to be using just a
  vehicle lap and shoulder belt,** are equally at risk.

So how can you protect children from potential air bag injury?

- To begin with, as discussed at length in Ch. 5, *Seat
  Belts and Child Safety Seats*, **the best place for
  children to be seated in a vehicle is in the
  back seat, preferably in the center** (if proper

restraints are available in that position, and the children are properly restrained for their age and size.)

- **Depending on the size of the child,** you should use a booster seat plus a lap/shoulder belt, or a lap/shoulder belt alone (for larger children). (Again, see Ch. 5, *Seat Belts and Child Safety Seats* for specifics.)

- **The vehicle seat needs to be pushed all the way back,** to maximize the distance between the child and the air bag.

- **The child needs to be sitting with his/her back against the seat back,** not wiggling around or leaning forward, **with as little slack as possible in the belt** in order to minimize forward movement in a crash.

Adults

Adults sitting in the **front passenger seat** of a vehicle equipped with a passenger-side air bag should:

- Be **properly restrained in a seat belt** (see Ch. 5, *Seat Belts and Child Safety Seats* for specifics.).

- **Sit at least 10 inches away** from the air bag compartment.

- **Avoid leaning or reaching forward.**

- **Remain seated against the vehicle seat back,** with **as little slack in the belt as possible** to minimize forward movement in a crash.

Short adults

Short adults in the **front passenger seat** of a vehicle equipped with a passenger-side air bag should *additionally*:

- **Move the seat as far *rearward* as possible.**

- **Tilt the seat back slightly** to help maximize the distance between their chest and the instrument panel (to 10 inches or more).

- **Refrain from moving around or sitting on the edge of the seat** — which could move their head too close to the air bag.

Elderly drivers and passengers

Elderly people, like all other drivers and front seat passengers, should be properly restrained and should move the seat as far rearward as possible, being careful to remain seated against the vehicle seat back and keeping the arms away from the area in which the air bag will deploy.

Tilt and Telescoping Steering Wheels

- **A tilt steering wheel should be tilted down** so that the air bag will deploy toward the chest and not the head.

- **Pregnant women should make sure the steering wheel is also tilted toward the chest,** not the abdomen or the head.

- **A telescoping steering wheel should be positioned so that it extends toward the driver as little as possible,** ensuring that the air bag has plenty of room to deploy.

Manual On-Off Switches for Air Bags

The National Highway Traffic Safety Administration **allows passenger air bag cut-off switches to be installed in vehicles with no rear seats or small rear seats.** Manufacturers may also use lower-powered air bags, which permits air bags to be depowered by 20 to 35 percent.

- **For a copy of the government rules** call the AutoSafety HotLine (800-424-9393) or visit the website (http://www.nhtsa.dot.gov).

- **All written comments/questions concerning air bags** should be addressed to the Administrator (NAO-10), NHTSA, 400 Seventh St., SW, Washington, DC 20590.

- Vehicle owners may request **authorization for a dealer to connect the air bag** (driver side, passenger side, or both) **to an on-off switch.**

  Vehicle owners can request an on-off switch by **filling out an agency request form** and submitting the form to the National Highway Traffic Safety Administration. (Website: www.nhtsa.dot.gov). Since the risk groups for *drivers* are different from those for *passengers*, **a separate certification** must be made on an agency request form **for each air bag** to be equipped with an on-off switch.

  If NHTSA approves a request, the agency will send the owner a letter authorizing the installation of one or more on-off switches in the owner's vehicle. The owner may **give the authorization letter to any dealer or repair business,** which may then install the switch(s).

NEVER ATTEMPT TO DISABLE THE AIR BAG YOURSELF. An air bag system is highly sophisticated and the air bag deploys with great force. Tampering with an air bag system is very risky. An inadvertent deployment can cause serious injuries.

Chapter 7

Tires, Part I

Type and Quality Make a Big Difference

Tires are one of the most important components of your car. **The quality of control you maintain over your vehicle is only as good as the tires that vehicle rolls on.** A car with outstanding handling qualities can have those qualities ruined by the installation of a poor set of tires.

So what do you need to know about the type and quality of the tires on your vehicle? Ideally, everything — from the chemical compound of the rubber, to the tire's construction (bias, bias-belted, or radial-ply), to the tread design (snow, all-weather, or conventional type passenger tires) — and more. Depending on your particular driving situation, all these characteristics in combination would either add to, or detract from, the optimum handling qualities of your vehicle.

TIRE TREAD DESIGN

First of all, **the purpose of tires is to create the road friction needed to do the things that can be done with cars, such as go, stop and turn.** And the more rubber in contact with the road, the more traction you have – up to a point. But your driving purpose and road conditions can dictate how

much and what kind of traction is necessary. Many emergency vehicles, such as police cruisers, for example have tires wider than more conventional passenger cars for this reason. And, if we could guarantee that no rain or snow would ever fall, and that roads would never get slippery, then we could use racing slicks (tires with no tread whatsoever) on all cars. (Racing tire rubbers include a compound that produces a maximum amount of friction with the road.) But if it rains, these tires are useless.

> **All tire designs are compromises of some sort, surrendering one advantage in order to gain another.**

All-Weather Tires

When the ground is covered with water, a good tire design swallows that water into the tread pattern and pushes it out to the sides of the tires. All-weather tires do this better than others. (Snow tires are completely different and require a different sort of design. See below.)

All-weather tires won't be as good as snow tires on some types of snow, and won't be better than performance tires in high-performance use, and may not last as long as a long-life passenger car tires — but all-weather tires are still better than all the others in matching the broad variety of driving conditions encountered in everyday driving.

Snow Tires

Snow tires may enable you to deal better with snowy conditions, but the most important drawback to snow tires comes in the area of driving performance — **they simply do not have the cornering performance of conventional tires.** A car equipped with snow tires in the rear and conventional tires up front is much more likely to go out of control in emergency situations. Even worse, **snow tires are not as good at stopping the car as conventional tires.**

Box 7-1. **New Tire Tread Simulation**

Tire companies such as Bridgestone Corporation, have strengthened winter tire design with computer simulation technology.

- The computer technology analyzes specific tread patterns in powering, stopping, and in turning a vehicle in slippery winter conditions.

- The new technology simulates the action of the various tread patterns as they compact and grip snow.

- Tire designers can thus view a simulated tread pattern in motion on a snowy road.

- These simulations even allow for quantifying the shear forces that arise between the tread grooves and the snow.

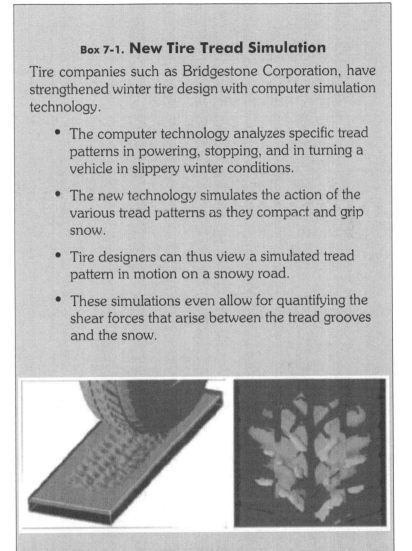

Figure 7-1. Tire Tread Simulation. Simulation of a tire in motion on snow (left) and a computer image of the distribution of the shearing forces that arise between the compacted snow and the tread (right). Photo courtesy of the National Highway Traffic Safety Administration.

In snowy areas, many cities and counties have
"snow emergency" regulations which are invoked
during heavy snowfalls. Check with authorities for
the rules in your area. Under some rules, motorists
are subject to fines if they block traffic and do not
have snow tires on their vehicles.

Chains and Studded Snow Tires

In areas where heavy snowfalls are frequent, many drivers
carry chains for use in emergencies, or have their tire dealer
apply studded snow tires for even greater traction.

* **Most states have time limits on use of studs,
  or ban them altogether**. Before applying studded
  tires, check the regulations in your area.

* **If you use chains, make sure they are the
  proper size and type for your tires.** Otherwise
  they may damage the tire sidewall and cause tire
  failure.

HOW TO DECODE A TIRE:
THE SIDEWALL STORY

**The US Department of Transportation requires tire
manufacturers to provide a wealth of information
molded into the sidewall of every tire.** Other useful
information, not government mandated, may appear there as
well.

    **The following examples will help you decode the
tires already on your — or any — vehicle.**
Understanding the codes will help make you an informed tire
purchaser and user, and will enable you to more easily follow
the "latest" news in tire reports and testing.

Typical Information on the Sidewall of a Passenger Car Tire

A tire sidewall shows, for example, the name of the tire, its size, whether it is tubeless or tube type, the maximum load and maximum inflation, an important safety warning, and much more information.

The trouble is, most of this information is in code.

For example, on the sidewall of a popular "P-metric" speed-rated auto tire, you'll find several codes:

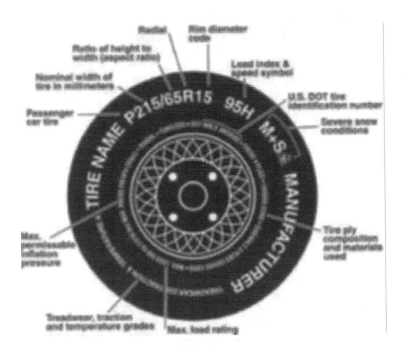

Figure 7-2. Sidewall Tire Information. Federal law requires tire manufacturers to place standardized information on the sidewall of all tires. This information identifies and describes the fundamental characteristics of the tire, and also provides a tire identification number for safety standard certification and in case of a recall. Illustration courtesy of the National Highway Traffic Safety Administration.

Example Code: P185/70R14

- The **"P"** indicates a **passenger-car** tire.

- The **"185"** is the nominal **width of the tire's cross-section in millimeters.**

- The **"70"** is the **aspect ratio** — the ratio of the sidewall's height to the tire's cross-sectional width. The sidewall in this example is 70% as high as the tire is wide.

- The **"R"** stands for **radial.** Virtually all passenger-car tires use radial-ply construction these days. (A **"B"** in place of the "R" means the tire is a **belted bias** construction. A **"D"** in place of the "R" means diagonal **"bias"** construction.)

  Tire longevity depends on the type of material the tire is belted with. In radial tire designs, nylon-belted tires last only half as long as their steel-belted counterparts.

- The **"14"** is the **diameter of the tire, in inches.**

Example Code: 87S

- The **"87"** is a code indicating the **maximum weight the tire can carry at its maximum rated speed** (This is not very useful information to most people.)

- The **"S"** is one of several possible **speed ratings**, or **the maximum speed that the tire is supposed to sustain without failure.** Some common speed ratings are: S, 112 mph; T, 118 mph; H, 130 mph; V, 149 mph; Z, 149 mph or more.

Example Code: Max. Load 730 kg (1609 lbs) 300 kPa (44 psi) Max. Press.

The maximum load is shown in lbs. (pounds) and in kg. (kilograms), and maximum pressure in PSI (pounds-per-square inch) and in kPa (kilopascals). Kilograms and kilopascals are metric units of measurement.

Example Code: Plies: tread 2 steel + 2 polyester + 1 nylon / sidewall: 2 polyester

The type of cord and number of plies is indicated for both the tread and the sidewalls.

Example Code: DOT Y7J6 CCD 053

- The letters **"DOT" certify compliance with all applicable safety standards** established by the U.S. Department of Transportation (DOT).

- The **"Y7J6"** is **an example DOT tire identification or serial number.** This serial number is a code with up to eleven digits that are a combination of numbers and letters.

- The **"CCD"** is **an example letter code indicating which plant made the tire.**

- The **"053"** is **an example three-digit date code** (in a rectangular depression), indicating when the tire was manufactured. The first two numbers are the week of the year. Hence, a date code of 053 would indicate the fifth week of 1993.

Example Code: TREADWEAR 420

The DOT requires tire manufacturers to grade passenger car tires based on three performance factors: Treadwear, Traction, and Temperature Resistance.

Tread-wear index or grade is a gauge of expected tread life, and is a comparative rating based on the wear rate of the tire when tested under controlled conditions on a specified government test track.

- **A tire graded 200** would wear twice as long on the government test course under specified test conditions as the "reference" one graded at 100.

- **A tread-wear rating of 420,** therefore, means that (in theory, at least) the tire should last 4.2 times as long as the reference tire.

- On typical tires, **a tread-wear index of 180 is quite low,** while **an index of 500 is quite high.**

- However, **it is erroneous to link treadwear grades with your projected tire mileage.** The relative performance of tires depends upon the actual conditions of their use, and may vary due to driving habits, type and condition of the vehicle, service practices, differences in road characteristics and climate.

> **Many observers within and without the tire industry have criticized the government-specified tests on several technical bases and because the tests are run by the tire makers themselves, without independent verification. The criticisms may be apt, but, as of now, the tread-wear index is the only game in town.**

Example Code: TRACTION A

The traction grades, from highest (the best) to lowest (the worst), are A, B, and C. They represent the tire's ability to stop on wet pavement as measured under controlled conditions on specified government test surfaces of asphalt and concrete.

- The traction score is an index of **straight-line stopping ability on a wet surface**. It's an undemanding test.

- **About half the passenger-car tires made are rated A.**

Example Code: *TEMPERATURE B*

The temperature grade is an index of a tire's ability to withstand the heat that high speeds, heavy loads, and hard driving generate.

The temperature grades are A (the highest), B and C, and represent the tire's resistance to the generation of heat when tested under controlled conditions on a specified indoor laboratory test wheel.

Typical Information on the Sidewall of a Light Truck Tire

- **"LT"** stands for Light Truck.

- **"LT235/85R16"** is the size designation for a metric light truck tire.

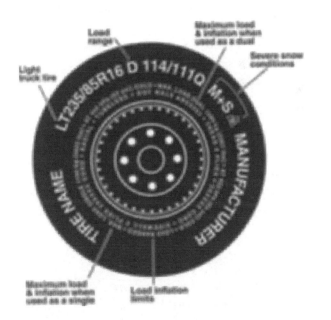

Figure 7-3. Sidewall Tire Information on Lite Truck Tires.
Lite truck tires have additional markings.
Illustration courtesy of the National Highway Traffic Safety Administration

- **"LOAD RANGED"** identifies the load and inflation limits.

- **"RADIAL"** identifies that the tire has a radial construction.

- **"MAX LOAD SINGLE 2623 lbs. AT 65 psi COLD"** indicates the maximum load rating of the tire and corresponding minimum cold inflation pressure for that load when used as a single.

  "MAX LOAD DUAL 2381 lbs. AT 65 psi COLD" would indicate the maximum load rating of the tire and corresponding minimum cold inflation pressure when used in a dual configuration.

  In simpler terms, when you have packed the maximum amount of weight allowed by the vehicle manufacturer, your inflation pressure should be whatever the recommendation marked on the tire suggests.

> **For normal operation, follow pressure recommendations in your owner's manual or on the vehicle placard.**

- **The other markings on the sidewall have the same meaning as described for the passenger car tire.**

REPLACEMENT TIRE SELECTION

When tires need to be replaced, don't guess what tire is right for your vehicle.

> **Tire types are specific for each type of vehicle.**

As we'll see later, in Ch. 13, *Maintaining Traction*, tires must be able to provide the friction necessary to handle the various maneuvers you put the vehicle through by accelerating, steering, and stopping — all usually at speed. And when you do this, you're transferring a lot of different forces to each tire. **The wrong tires on your vehicle could mean they simply won't be able to hold the road as they were designed to.** And you'd probably find this out in a big hurry in an emergency situation.

To find out what type of tire you need for your vehicle, first look at the tire placard.

> **The tire placard (or sticker) is attached to the vehicle — on the door edge, door post, or glove compartment.**

If your vehicle doesn't have a placard, **check the owner's manual.**

Tire Size and Construction

As you will see, that placard tells you **the size and type of the tires which were on the vehicle as original equipment.**

- Tires should **always be replaced with the same size designation**, or *approved options*, as recommended by the automobile or tire manufacturer.

- **Never choose a smaller size** with less load carrying capacity than the size on the tire placard.

Speed Rating

Some tires are now marked with letters to indicate their speed rating, based on laboratory tests which relate to performance on the road. (See p. 68)

- If the vehicle manual specifies speed-rated tires, **the replacement tires must have the same or**

higher speed rating to maintain vehicle speed capability.

• If tires with different speed ratings are mounted on the same vehicle, **the tire or tires with the lowest rating will limit permissible tire-related vehicle speed.**

When buying new tires, be sure your name, address and tire identification number (DOT code) are recorded and returned to the tire manufacturer or his record-keeping designee.

Tire registration enables the manufacturer to notify you in the event of a recall.

TIRE MOUNTING — DO'S AND DON'T'S

It is preferred that all four tires be of the same size, speed rating, and construction (radial or non-radial). But in some instances it may be necessary to use **tires that do not match.** Here are some guidelines:

• **Match tire size and construction designations in pairs on an axle** (or four tires in dual application), except for use of a temporary spare tire.

• If **two radial and two non-radial tires** are used on a vehicle, put the radials on the rear.

• If **two radial and two non-radial tires** are used on a vehicle equipped with **dual rear tires**, the radials may be used on either axle.

Never mix radial and non-radial on the same axle except for use of a temporary spare tire.

- **Snow tires** should be applied in pairs (or as duals) to the *drive* axle (whether front or rear) or to all four positions.

- Never put **non-radial snow tires** on the rear if radials are on the front, except when the vehicle has duals on the rear.

- If **studded snow tires** are used on the front axle, studded tires must also be used on the rear axle.

- Match all tire sizes and constructions on **four-wheel drive vehicles.**

Only specially trained persons should demount or mount tires. An explosion of a tire and wheel assembly can result from improper or careless mounting procedures.

Chapter 8

Tires, Part II[1]

Care and Maintenance Make an Even Bigger Difference

Tires must be treated with care, for there are many factors that can affect their life and performance — weather, driving habits, inflation pressure, vehicle alignment and wheel balance, and vehicle loading.

PROPER TIRE INFLATION PRESSURE

One of the most important maintenance procedures is checking your tires — **including the spare** — for proper inflation pressure.

With the right amount of air pressure, your tires wear longer, save fuel, and help prevent accidents. The "right amount" of air is the pressure specified by the vehicle manufacturer for the front and rear tires on your particular model car or light truck.

The Correct Air Pressure

The correct air pressure (cold tire pressure) is shown on the tire placard (or sticker) attached to the vehicle — the door edge, door post, or glove box door. If your vehicle doesn't have a placard, check the owner's manual or consult with the vehicle or tire manufacturer for the proper inflation.

---

[1] Sections in this chapter marked with * are copyright Shell Oil Company materials, used with permission.

Inflation pressures are determined by the auto maker based on the car's weight and the anticipated load it will carry. However, it is difficult for the car builders to figure out exactly how much weight will be transferred to the front of the car during heavy braking. So, although a *perfect* tire pressure for all conditions is nearly impossible to come up with, the indicated psi is the one you should follow for most driving situations.

> **REMEMBER: The tire pressure number that is molded into the sidewall of a tire is the tire *maximum* — not the *recommended* — inflation pressure. (See pp. 67, 68)**

Freeway or expressway driving and tire inflation

Those who spend a lot of time in prolonged freeway or expressway driving (that is, routinely drive at a sustained speed of 60 mph) should *increase* tire pressure over the manufacturer's recommended pressure — **as long as that pressure doesn't exceed the maximum psi figure printed on the tire sidewall.**

> 4.0 psi increase in radial tires
>
> 5.5 psi increase in bias belted tires
>
> 7.0 psi increase in bias tires

Cold/hot weather driving and tire inflation

Many parts of the U.S. have cold weather driving conditions at least part of the year. Here are some things you should know about cold weather driving and its effects on tire inflation:

- **Every time the outside temperature drops 10 degrees Fahrenheit, the air pressure inside your tires goes down about one (1) pound per square inch.** You should check your tire pressures frequently during cold weather and add the necessary air to keep them at recommended levels of inflation at all times.

- Similarly, **pressure may increase when the temperature rises.**

- **Never reduce tire pressures in an attempt to increase traction on snow or ice.** It doesn't work and your tires will be so seriously underinflated that driving will damage them.

The new D-metric tires and tire inflation

If you are driving a car equipped with a set of the new D-metric tires (which will eventually replace the alpha-numeric size tires), you should know that **the D-metric tire pressures can be exceeded by two or three psi over the recommended pressures listed in the owner's manual** or on the tire placard. Not only can these pressures be exceeded by a small amount, D-metric tires are inflated to a higher pressure overall.

Keeping Tires at Proper Pressure Is Easy

It's vitally important to keep track of the amount of air in your tires — including the spare.

How often should you check your tire inflation pressure? Ideally, you should check the pressure:

- At least once a month

- When the temperature changes

- Before, during, and after every long trip

Check your tires when they are COLD — that is, when your vehicle has not been used for at least three hours.

Tire pressure gauges are inexpensive and fit in a pocket. There are many models to choose from. You can pick one up at most service stations and auto parts stores. **Compressed air is available at almost every gas station.**

> The hardest part to keeping tires properly inflated is simply taking the few moments required to do the job.

THE PERILS OF IMPROPER INFLATION

If you don't take proper care of your tires, the results can be serious.

* **Under- or overinflation can cause tire failure/explosion of tire/rim assembly.** In fact, most manufacturers now mold a safety warning on the sidewall of the tire. It points out that serious injury may result from tire failure due to underinflation or overloading:

> **WARNING: Serious injury may result from:**
> *** Tire failure due to underinflation/ overloading. Follow owner's manual or tire placard in vehicle.**
> *** Explosion of tire/rim assembly.**

* It is far **easier to go out of control on underinflated tires.**

   Tire pressure affects the tire's ability to corner. The sharper the turn required by a corner, the more effect tire pressure has. This is due to the fact that a sharp turn puts more stress on a tire than a gentle turn, and an underinflated tire accepts less stress before losing its grip on the pavement and going out of control. For example, a tire rated for inflation to 32 psi but only carrying 24 psi loses 10 percent of its handling capability on sharp turns. (See p. 144)

A car is a weight-bearing machine. Every time you move the controls, you are shifting weight throughout the vehicle (see p. 119). These shifts are all eventually felt at the tires — and the tires' ability to bear that weight is dependent on the tire pressures.

- **Underinflation prematurely wears tires.** The rule of thumb is that **a single pound of underinflation takes 500 miles off a tire's life.** Most tires only last 70 percent of their design life, thanks to underinflation.

- **Tire pressures affect fuel consumption.** Properly inflated tires are part of the fuel economy equation. If a tire intended to be inflated to 32 psi is inflated to 24 psi, the result is a 20 percent boost in fuel consumption. This is due to the fact that a properly inflated tire offers less rolling resistance than one that's underinflated, so it requires more energy to roll an underinflated tire than one with the proper amount of air in it, and in an automobile, energy is gasoline. **If the tires on your car aren't properly inflated, you're wasting hundreds of miles' worth of gasoline.**

On the average, cars lose mileage at the rate of about a half a mile per gallon if the tires fall six pounds below a recommended inflation (of 25 pounds per square inch [psi]).

- Underinflated tires also exhibit **less overall durability** and can be **more easily damaged.**

- **Tire type makes a difference.** Radial tires have two-thirds the rolling resistance of a cross- or bias-ply tire. Over 40,000 miles, a properly inflated radial tire pays for itself.

SYMPTOMS OF "SICK" TIRES

When tires get "sick," they show their drivers an abundant number of symptoms in plenty of time for the tires to be "cured." By learning to read the early warning signs, you can prevent situations that both shorten tire life by thousands of miles, and that make those tires unsafe to drive on.

- As we have said, when a tire is **underinflated,** most of its road contact is on the outer tread ribs, causing the outside edge of the tire to wear faster than the middle.

- With **overinflation,** the opposite wear pattern appears. The center tread area bulges out slightly, causing it to wear faster than the outer ribs.

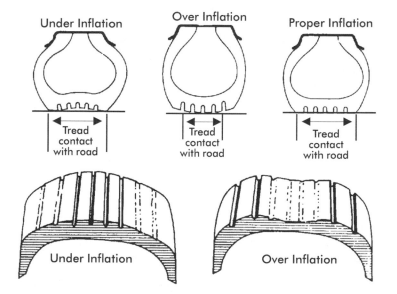

Figure 8-1. How Tires Look with Various Amounts of Inflation.

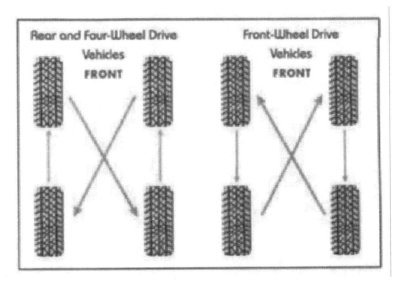

Figure 8-2. Common Correct Tire Rotation Patterns.
Illustration courtesy The Department of Transportation,
National Highway Traffic Safety Administration

PROPER TIRE ROTATION

For maximum mileage and uniform tire wear, **rotate your tires every 5,000-6,000 miles,** and be sure to **follow the correct rotation pattern for your vehicle** as specified in your owner's manual

WORN TIRES

Worn tires are trouble. If you're driving on worn tires, you're **driving without the tread depth that controls stopping, acceleration, and cornering.** When driving on worn tires, you've thrown away some of the control you should have over your vehicle.

- Worn tires are **prone to hydroplaning** (see p. 252), are much **more susceptible to puncture** and could otherwise be hazardous to your health.

Studies by several auto safety organizations, among them the National Bureau of Standards, showed that **cars riding on tires with less than one-sixteenth of an inch of tread are up to 44 times more likely to experience a blow-out.**

- More than just unsafe, **worn tires are often illegal.** The Tire Industry Safety Council reports that 30 states now have laws on the books requiring that automobile tires have **at least one-sixteenth of an inch of tread** — any less and the driver is issued a summons. (See Box 8-2, p. 87 for quick tips on measuring tread depth.)

TIRE ABUSE — YOURS AND NATURE'S

Wheel Spinning

Picture it: **Your car is stuck in mud or in snow, or on a patch of ice**. If your first reaction is to shove the "pedal to the metal" and spin the tire free, you're only asking for more trouble — some of it quite serious.

A spinning tire creates friction, producing tremendous amounts of heat — and heat is a tire's worst enemy. This heat, combined with the centrifugal forces produced by spinning, could cause the tire to fail.

> **The worst case scenario for this situation is a catastrophic tire failure, resulting in tire detonation and the possibility of a dangerous shower of hot rubber!**

In such a situation, most drivers don't realize just how fast their tires are spinning.

> **A spinning tire's speed is often *twice* that displayed on the speedometer.**

Here's why: if one tire is spinning and the other is in a situation that doesn't allow it to spin, the spinnable tire will receive the engine's total power output because the car's differential will transfer the engine's power to the point of least resistance. So, if the speedometer reads 60 mph, the tire is really spinning at 120 mph!

> **Do not exceed 35 mph *speedometer* speed — and make sure *no one* stands near the spinning tire.**

As if all this tire danger weren't bad enough, **spinning the tires doesn't get the car free.**

- For one thing, **spinning the tires makes the road surface slicker** by melting snow which then refreezes as ice and also creates ruts that can further complicate the process of freeing the car.

- For another, **increased tire speed is not going to create traction.** Peak traction is generated at very low speeds. Once a tire is spinning 15 percent faster than the car is moving, maximum traction has been lost.

> **To free a trapped car, briefly rock the vehicle, tow it, or apply a traction aid such as sand or kitty litter to the surface under the tire.**

Driving Speed

The faster you drive, the faster you'll wear out your tires. As a car is driven, the rear wheels press down on the pavement. At 30 mph, the rear tires exert a 5 horse power (hp) push against the pavement. At 50 mph, some 15 hp are exerted, and by 70 mph, this figure grows to 38 hp.

Temperature and Temperature Changes

Temperature also has an extreme effect on tires. *Low* temperatures, or *changes* in temperature wear tires out faster.

Box 8-1. Your Driving Habits and Tire "Health"*

Perhaps the easiest factor to control is your driving behavior. Simply following these good driving habits will help extend the life of your tires:

- **Obey posted speed limits.**

- **Avoid fast starts, stops and turns.**

- **Avoid potholes and other objects** on the road.

- **Do not run over curbs or hit your tires against the curb** when parking.

- **Do not overload your vehicle.** Refer to your vehicle's tire information or owner's manual for the maximum recommended load.

- Tests have shown that **a change from a winter temperature such as 41 degrees** Fahrenheit **to a hot summer day temperature of 95 degrees** Fahrenheit **increases tire wear 400 percent,** all other conditions being equal.

Box 8-2. Checklist to
Help Your Tires Last Longer*

☑ **PRESSURE** - One-fourth of all cars and one-third of all light trucks have at least one substantially underinflated tire. Underinflated tires can cause blowouts and tire failure, which can lead to serious accidents. And appearances can be deceiving - a tire can lose up to half of its air pressure and not appear to be flat. Overinflation, on the other hand, puts unnecessary stress on tires, which can result in irregular tread wear. Check tire inflation with an accurate gauge. They can be found in any auto parts store and most service stations.

☑ **ALIGNMENT** - Improper alignment of your car's steering mechanisms - including the front and rear tires and the steering wheel - can reduce the lifespan of your tires by thousands of miles. Have a tire dealer check the alignment if you notice:

- Excessive or uneven tire wear
- The steering wheel "pulling" to the right or the left
- A feeling of "looseness" or "wandering"
- Steering wheel vibration
- The steering wheel is not centered when the car is moving straight ahead

☑ **ROTATION** - If you fail to rotate your tires, the front tires may last only 10,000 - 20,000 miles, while the rear tires will last 50,000 - 80,000 miles. Therefore, to achieve more uniform wear, experts recommend that you have your tires rotated every 6,000 miles. Refer to your vehicle's owner's manual for correct pattern rotation. Common patterns include straight forward and straight back or crisscrossed.

☑ **TREAD** - Advanced and unusual wear can reduce the ability of tread to grip the road in adverse conditions - especially on wet roads. When checking tires, look for uneven wear, high and low areas, bubbling or excessively smooth areas, as well as cuts or foreign objects in your tires.

- **Tires must be replaced when tread has worn down to 1/16 of an inch.** *Quick tip:* If you don't have a measurement device handy, you can simply use a penny to check tread depth. Insert a penny with the head pointed down into the tread groove. If you can see all of Lincoln's head, your tires need to be replaced.
- **When shopping for new tires, it is usually best to replace all four at the same time** — *if* you have been rotating your tires as recommended. You also should think about the type of driving you do most often and choose tires that are right for you.

IN THE NEXT TWO CHAPTERS, we consider some general maintenance rules for your vehicle — what to check or have checked, and how often. And a convenient ***Ten-Minute Checklist*** covers 17 items to check, and when to check them.

Chapter 9

Smart Car Care:

Tips for Keeping Your Vehicle Safe and on the Road[1]

Stick to Your Routine (Maintenance)

Next to a home, a vehicle is probably the most expensive purchase people make. That's why it makes good economic sense for owners to take proper care of their vehicles through preventive and routine maintenance. Following the quick and simple procedures outlined in this chapter will not only add years to the life of your vehicle, but will help keep it operating in a safe and cost-efficient manner. Plus, finding and fixing a smaller problem before it turns into a major problem can help save you a bundle.

> **Note: This chapter is intended to provide a general overview of routine maintenance. Because there are so many different makes and models of vehicles and auto parts and accessories, recommended procedures may vary. Please consult your owner's manual or the product manufacturers for recommendations.**

Keep Your Vehicle a Well-Oiled Machine

A regular oil change is the service most likely to prolong the life of your vehicle; yet, recent nationwide vehicle inspections

---

[1] Copyright Shell Oil Company material reproduced with permission. Written with assistance from the National Highway Traffic Safety Administration (NHTSA), the National Institute for Automotive Service Excellence (ASE), the Rubber Manufacturers Association, and the AAA Foundation for Traffic Safety.

found that 22 percent of vehicles have low or dirty engine oil, indicating that many motorists fail to perform this important task. Not changing your oil for lengthy periods of time will cause additives in the oil to break down, leading to increased wear and tear on your engine.

To keep your vehicle running smoothly:

- Check the oil level regularly.

- Change the oil every 3,000 miles or every three months, whichever comes first, unless your manufacturer recommends otherwise. Some newer vehicles need less frequent oil changes.

- Replace the oil filter with every change.

- For an accurate reading of your oil level, shut off the engine, remove the dipstick, wipe it with a clean cloth or paper towel and then reinsert it. Remove the dipstick again to "read" the oil level.

Go with the Flow: Your Vehicle's Fluids

Engine oil is not the only fluid your vehicle needs to run properly. Other vital fluids include brake fluid, power steering fluid, transmission fluid, and coolant. Checking them on a regular basis can prevent breakdowns and costly repairs.

Your owner's manual can show you where fluids are contained, exactly how to check them, the type your vehicle uses and how much should be in each "reservoir." (See Box 9-1, p. 91 and Ch. 10, *Know Your Car: The Ten-Minute Checklist* for suggestions on frequency of fluid checks and how to identify leaks.)

Know the Positives and Negatives of Your Battery

Cars run on three components: fuel, air, and electricity. Many people never think of vehicles as being "electronic," but they are complex machines with many electronic components, ranging from the radio to on-board computers. The battery is

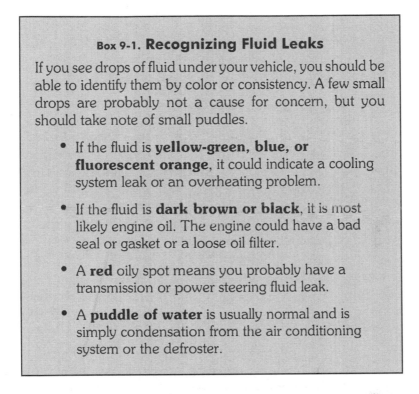

Box 9-1. **Recognizing Fluid Leaks**

If you see drops of fluid under your vehicle, you should be able to identify them by color or consistency. A few small drops are probably not a cause for concern, but you should take note of small puddles.

- If the fluid is **yellow-green, blue, or fluorescent orange**, it could indicate a cooling system leak or an overheating problem.

- If the fluid is **dark brown or black**, it is most likely engine oil. The engine could have a bad seal or gasket or a loose oil filter.

- A **red** oily spot means you probably have a transmission or power steering fluid leak.

- A **puddle of water** is usually normal and is simply condensation from the air conditioning system or the defroster.

the primary source of power for these electronic components, so it is important to make sure it is working properly.

Batteries can fail for a number of reasons, including insecure mounting, frequent "deep cycling" (the recharging of a dead battery) and dirty or poor connections.

Here are some ways to help prevent your battery from failing and leaving you stranded:

- **Have the battery checked with every oil change.**

- **Cables should be securely attached and free of corrosion.** You can clean the battery terminals and case with a mixture of baking soda and water.

- **Don't wait until your battery fails before you
  replace it.** Vehicles that are three years old or older
  are most likely to experience battery failure.

Start Your Car Correctly

**You probably don't think much about how to start
your car. You get in, turn the key, and go-until the
time you get in the car and the car does not start.**
There is a right way and a wrong way to start your car, and
knowing the right way to start your car, though, will increase the
life your car. Cold starts are the bad for cars cold starts are
starting your car for the first time in the morning, or when the
engine has been off for a while.

**First, set the parking brake by placing your foot
firmly on the pedal, or pulling up firmly on the lever.**
John Totz, district service manager for the Ford Motor
Company, advises also making sure that all accessories are off
so full electrical power can be delivered to the starting system.

**Next, in a car with an automatic transmission, put
the car in "park" or "neutral" to disengage the
starter interlock system**. In a car with manual transmission,
depress the clutch fully and put the car in neutral. On carburetor
cars, if the temperature is below freezing or if the engine hasn't
been started in at least two days, press the gas two or three
times to make the initial fuel mixture "richer"-that is, to increase
the proportion of gas in the gas-air combination.

**Fuel-injected cars are computer controlled, so you
shouldn't touch the gas pedal at all.** "In fact," says Mike
Michels of the Toyota Motor Company of America, "hitting the
gas only confuses the computer."

**Finally, turn the key. Don't press or pump the gas
pedal while turning the key in a fuel- injected car.** In
a carbureted car, press the accelerator down to one-quarter to
one half of the way. Release the gas immediately when the car
starts.

In normal weather the car should start in four seconds. At temperatures below freezing, the car should start in 10 seconds. Release the key from start position as soon as the car starts. "Do not crank the car for more than 30 seconds, or the starter motor may overheat," warns Tutz.

No matter what kind of car you have, fuel-injected or carbureted, automatic or manual, you don't need a warm up. Once the engine starts, drive off gently. If you can't, you need repairs.

Long warm-ups reduce gas mileage, and long periods at fast idle (10 minutes or more) will damage the catalytic converter. On the other hand, avoid putting undo stress on the engine until the oil has had the opportunity to circulate to all engine parts. (If you're using the proper weight of oil, (that should be no more than a few seconds.) Never race an engine-carbureted or fuel-injected-right after starting, no matter how impatient you are to "warm it up". Michels notes that 90 percent of all engine wear occurs during the first few minutes. If the car doesn't start on the first try, release the ignition, let the car sit for a few seconds and try again. If it still doesn't start, wait several minutes before trying again.

If the engine should flood press the accelerator down all the way to the floor and hold it. On a fuel-injected car this sends a message to the computer that the car is flooded, and the computer in turn shuts off all fuel. On a carbureted car, pressing the accelerator all the way to the floor allows more air to pass through the manifold, evaporating the excess gas. Don't pump the accelerator while you crank the engine. If these procedures don't work, your car may need maintenance. "Computer-controlled fuel injection rarely floods the engine," says Michels, "unless there is some malfunction with the fuel delivery system."

If you maintain your car well, you shouldn't have to change your starting procedure as the car gets older. However, as the miles add up, you may find that a variation of the procedure produces faster starts. That usually indicates that some part of the starting system or the other system is wearing out or beginning to fail.

Check Wipers & Washer Fluid Intermittently

Like other components, windshield wipers also wear out and need to be replaced. Not being able to see clearly while driving is very dangerous. In fact, 90 percent of all driving decisions made are based solely on visual cues. That's why car care experts recommend **wipers be changed once a year for cars that are parked inside and two to three times a year for cars that are parked outside.** A good rule of thumb to follow is: "change your clocks, change your wipers." (See Ch. 4, *Windshields and Mirrors* for additional discussion on wipers.) Here are some other tips:

- **You can tell when a blade is becoming worn** out if it just streaks and smears the water rather than wiping it away.

- **Inspect the wiper blades whenever you clean your windshield.** Do not wait until the rubber is worn or brittle to replace them.

- **Most of the time, only the rubber squeegee,** usually called the "44 refill," **needs to be replaced.**

- **When buying a blade,** take the old rubber squeegee with you to the store so you can compare sizes.

- **When refilling the windshield washer fluid,** use some of the fluid to clean the wiper blades.

Light the Way to Safer Driving

Lights are one of your vehicle's most important safety features. They help you and other drivers make decisions based on visual cues. However, recent statistics indicate that 20 percent of vehicles tested are operating with at least one external light not functioning. Therefore, it is important to check your lights often to make sure they are clean and in good working order. This includes headlights (both low and high beams), parking lights, blinkers, taillights, and brake lights.

- If any of these lights is not in working order, you can be ticketed.

- Typically, if any of these lights is not working, all you will need is an inexpensive bulb or fuse.

Help Your Tires Tread Lightly

(Because there are many factors that affect the life of your tires — and because properly maintained tires are *fundamental* to vehicle control and safety — **an entire chapter is devoted to a discussion of their care and maintenance.** (See Ch. 8, *Tires, Part II: Care and Maintenance Make an Even Bigger Difference.*)

Conserve Fuel

Non-commercial vehicles in the United States consume close to 90 billion gallons of gasoline each year — that's 661 gallons per car. While many of the tips in this chapter will help increase your vehicle's fuel mileage, there is even more you can do to maximize fuel efficiency:

- **Avoid high speeds.** Fuel efficiency decreases significantly at speeds in excess of 55 miles per hour. Reducing your speed from 62 mph to 55 mph reduces fuel consumption by 10 percent.

- **Avoid excessive idling.** If you must warm up the engine, one to three minutes should be sufficient.

- **Don't rev the engine;** it wastes gas and may cause engine damage.

- **Drive smoothly** and **avoid sudden braking and starting.**

- **Minimize drag** by keeping your car clean, driving with windows and sunroofs closed, and removing roof and rear racks. Having a clean car can reduce drag by as much as 12 percent.

- **Be sure to replace the gas cap tightly** to prevent gasoline from evaporating.

- **During the summer, fuel your car early in the morning or late in the evening.** Heat expands gasoline, so you'll spend more money for less gasoline if you refuel during the afternoon.

While the tips in this chapter will help lengthen the life of your vehicle and enhance the safety of its occupants, they are not a substitute for the recommendations of a qualified auto technician or your vehicle's owner's manual.

Though preventive maintenance will minimize the chance for breakdowns, it is important to be prepared by traveling with an appropriately-stocked "emergency kit," and by knowing what to do to get help and stay safe if your car breaks down on the road.

For a full discussion of these topics, see Ch. 11, *Your Glove Compartment and Trunk: Keep Them Well Stocked,* and Ch. 28, *Roadside Breakdown: How to Deal with Roadside Emergencies.*

Chapter 10

Know Your Car:
The Ten-Minute Checklist[1]

Air Filter

- Check every two to three months.
- A dirty air filter reduces gas mileage and the lifespan of your motor.
- Replace it when it is dirty or during your annual engine performance check.
- If you drive in very dusty conditions, you may need to check your air filter more frequently.

Battery

- Have the battery checked with every oil change and periodically check cables for corrosion.
- Use of felt rings (positioned around the battery post under the clamp) — available at any auto parts store — will reduce corrosion.
- Consider replacing your battery if it is three years old or older.

Belts and Hoses

- Check monthly.
- If your belts or hoses look or feel hard, spongy, cracked or shiny, they should be replaced right away.
- It's best to leave the replacement to an expert.
- Also, be on the lookout for loose, cracked or missing clamps.

---

[1] Copyright Shell Oil Company material, reproduced with permission.

Brake Fluid

- Check monthly.
- First, wipe any dirt from the master brake cylinder cover. Then remove the cover.
- If you need fluid, add the proper type (refer to your owner's manual) and check for possible leaks. Don't overfill.

Brake System

- Experts recommend having your brake system thoroughly inspected once a year or every 12,000 miles, whichever comes first.

Coolant/ Antifreeze

- Check frequently.
- You should be able to see the level of coolant in the reservoir.
- Follow the manufacturer's instructions to determine if the level is low.
- If necessary, add coolant to the reservoir — NOT the radiator — and fill to the proper level.

Engine Oil

- Check oil level regularly (twice a month is ideal).
- Have the oil (and oil filter) changed every three months or every 3,000 miles, whichever comes first, unless your vehicle's manufacturer specifies otherwise.

Lights

- Check regularly to ensure they are clean and in good working order.
- Remember to check:
- Headlights
- Taillights
- Brake lights
- Turn signals

Power Steering Fluid

- Check monthly using the reservoir dipstick.
- If low, add the proper type of fluid (refer to your owner's manual).
- Inspect the pump and hoses for leaks.

Shock Absorbers

- Test once every two to three months by bouncing your car up and down; when you step away, the car should stop bouncing.
- Always replace shock absorbers in pairs.

Tire Pressure

- Check monthly when tires are cold — that is, when they have not been used for at least three hours — using a tire gauge.
- For proper tire inflation, refer to your owner's manual or the label on the driver's side door edge or in the glove compartment of your vehicle.
- The number molded into the sidewall of your tires is the maximum, not the recommended, tire pressure.

Wheel Alignment

- Have the alignment checked immediately if the vehicle feels "loose," "pulls" to one side or if there is uneven tire wear.

Tire Rotation

- Have your tires rotated approximately every 6,000 miles or with every other oil change.

Tire Tread

- Look for uneven wear, separation or excessive smoothness.

- Replace tires immediately if the tread has worn down to 1/16 of an inch or less.

- Use a measuring device or the "penny test": Insert a penny with the head pointed down into the tread groove. If you can see all of Lincoln's head, your tires need to be replaced.

Transmission Fluid

- **Automatic**:

  ü Check your owner's manual for the exact procedure.

  ü Most vehicles should be running at normal operating temperature with the parking brake firmly set.

  ü Then shift the transmission into park or neutral (refer to the owner's manual or look on the dipstick), remove the dipstick, wipe it clean, fully reinsert it and remove it again.

  ü Read the fluid level and add fluid of the recommended type as needed.

- **Manual:**

  ü Checking the fluid on a manual transmission is better left to a service professional, as the car must often be raised.

Washer Fluid

- Check the washer fluid reservoir regularly and add fluid as needed.

Wiper Blades

- Check at least twice each year for signs of wear.
- Replace if wipers streak or smear.
- Don't wait until the rubber is brittle or worn.

IN THE NEXT CHAPTER, we look at what should be inside every safe driver's glove compartment and trunk. You may never have cause to use some of the items — but if you ever have an emergency on the road, you'll be more than glad you have them.

Chapter 11

The Glove Compartment and Trunk:

Keep Them Well Stocked for Safety

Our vehicle's glove compartment and trunk are often like our closets at home.

- **Some of us have them stocked to the gills with everything imaginable** — a lot of it often just "stuff" and "junk" we don't even know we have, much less need.

- **These days, some of us carry our "offices," "tool shops," or our complete collection of gym and sports items in our trunks — or even the overflow from our closets or garages.** (A friend's neighbor keeps her *vacuum cleaner* in her trunk — no room for it in her small apartment!)

- **Others have hardly *anything* in their glove compartments or trunks.** You know, those who like to be extra neat or who don't think there's anything they'll ever need in their car besides themselves and their passengers, or who think it's senseless to carry things they don't know how to use — and never would.

- And many drivers **mistakenly think that if they have a valid motor club "road service" card, that *that's* all they'll ever need in an emergency.**

- And some even **think they'll NEVER be involved in a road side emergency,** however minor.

But all of these practices and attitudes are very short-sighted. Emergencies — large and small — happen on the road every day (as we'll see in Chs. 22-30). You never know if you'll be faced with, or involved in, a breakdown, an accident, or bad weather. And you may be stuck in a situation or location where "road service" can't help.

Safe drivers make sure they are prepared for emergency situations by equipping their vehicles with an "emergency supply kit" — stocked with the tools, safety, and first-aid items that you — or someone else — can use to help you with a roadside emergency.

The following lists suggest articles you should have in your vehicle at all times[1] — some in the glove compartment, some in the trunk — *wherever* you can *readily* get your hands on them if, and when, you need them.

When putting together your kit, consider the area of the country in which you drive and *ADD* ITEMS ACCORDINGLY.

If possible, always carry a CELL PHONE while on the road.

And, always remember to carry CHANGE FOR A PAY PHONE — because cell phones can lose connections, run out of power, or just not have service where you are stuck.

---

[1] These lists were compiled from Shell Oil Company materials (used with permission, and originally written in cooperation with the American Red Cross, the Federal Highway Administration, the National Crime Prevention Council, and the National Institute for Automotive Service.)

WHAT TO CARRY IN THE GLOVE COMPARTMENT
in Case of a Breakdown

- ☑ The vehicle's *User's Manual*
- ☑ "Call Police" sign (often found on the back of store-bought sunshades)
- ☑ Bright handkerchief or cloth
- ☑ Telephone numbers of people to call in an emergency
- ☑ Pen or marker and message pad
- ☑ Flashlight and extra batteries (check batteries often to be sure they work)
- ☑ Automobile registration
- ☑ Insurance documents
- ☑ Copy of health insurance card
- ☑ Emergency medical alert information, if applicable

WHAT TO CARRY IN YOUR TRUNK

- ☑ Flares or reflective devices (flares burn very hot; use only if you know how to safely light and place them)

> **WARNING: When setting out flares, be certain you do not put them close to brush, grass, or debris that can catch on fire. You don't want to turn the original emergency into an even bigger one!**

- ☑ Jack and lug wrench (practice using at home following your owner's manual)
- ☑ Spare tire properly inflated (check often)
- ☑ Tool kit (adjustable wrench, insulated pliers, two insulated screwdrivers [one Phillips head, one standard]; duct tape; fuse puller)
- ☑ Jumper cables

> **WARNING: Jumper cables can be
> dangerous if used improperly. See Ch. 25,
> *Roadside Breakdown*, p. 276, for
> instructions and cautions.**

☑ Fire extinguisher — unexpired and securely stored with the correct charge (make sure it's the right type and that you know when and how to use it properly)

> **See Box 11-1, p. 107 for warnings and
> some specifics that you should be aware of
> before using a fire extinguisher on an
> automobile fire.**

☑ Extra light fuses (check size in *Owner's Manual*)
☑ A spare fan belt (even if you can't put it on yourself, you'll be ready with the right size when the tow truck arrives; check *Owner's Manual* for correct size)
☑ Tire repair canister (sealant-inflator)
☑ Strong rope or tow chain
☑ All-purpose wire (to lash down a sprung trunk, door, whatever)
☑ Flashlight/spotlight and extra batteries (check batteries often to be sure they work)
☑ Swiss Army-style knife
☑ At least one quart of oil (check type in *Owner's Manual*)
☑ First aid kit — (see list on p. 108 for contents)
☑ Blankets — regular and solar
☑ Empty, approved gas container
☑ Siphon
☑ Umbrella, poncho or raincoat
☑ Gloves
☑ Bottled drinking water — at least a gallon (replace every year or when shelf date expires)
☑ Non-perishable, easy-open food items

Box 11-1. Fire Extinguishers and Automotive Fires*

A fire extinguisher is a handy device to have in your trunk — but it is essential that you have the right type and that you know not only how to use it safely, but when and when *NOT* to use it.

☑ **The best all-around fire extinguisher for automobiles** would be an **"ABC Dry Chemical" with a UL rating of 3A:40B:C.** This extinguisher usually contains 5 lbs. of extinguishing agent. It is rated to put out Class A fires (ordinary combustibles), Class B fires (flammable liquids), and Class C fires (fires in electrical equipment).

☑ The extinguisher should be **securely mounted in its bracket** and **kept accessible for immediate use.** It should be **checked every six months** to ensure that it has proper pressure and is not damaged.

☑ Be sure to **carefully read and understand the operating instructions. ONLY IF YOU FEEL CONFIDENT ABOUT THE USE OF FIRE EXTINGUISHERS AND *WHEN* TO USE ONE SHOULD YOU ATTEMPT TO USE ONE ON AN AUTOMOBILE FIRE.**

☑ Consider that **aside from the fuel in the vehicle, all of the plastics used in modern automobiles are also highly flammable.** Keep in mind that the **smoke from a burning automobile is *extremely toxic*** and breathing the smoke could have serious consequences.

☑ **A fire that appears small can rapidly grow out of control.** In any event, **NOTIFY THE LOCAL FIRE DEPARTMENT AS SOON AS POSSIBLE** so that they can begin their response. The longer you wait to notify them, the longer the fire has to get out of control.

☑ **Fires near or involving the gas tank are especially dangerous** and should be left to the fire department to handle.

☑ **If the fire is in the engine compartment,** it will be necessary to open the hood to effect extinguishment. However, opening the hood can be *very* dangerous as fresh air will be introduced and may make the fire flare up and burn you.

☑ **If the fire is producing large volumes of smoke, and/or flames are shooting out of the engine compartment,** it is best to leave the hood closed and await the arrival of the fire department.

☑ **Special note regarding newer alternate-fueled and hybrid automobiles.** Fires in these types of automobiles can be *especially* hazardous and should be left to the fire department to extinguish.

*Information provided by Bryan T. Sammartino, NJ Level II Fire Instructor

WHAT TO KEEP IN A FIRST AID KIT

- Sterile adhesive bandages
- 2" and 4" sterile gauze pads
- Gauze rolls
- Hypoallergenic adhesive tape
- Hypoallergenic surgical gloves
- Triangular bandages
- 2" and 3" sterile bandages
- Scissors
- Tweezers
- Mouth barrier
- Antiseptic
- Thermometer
- Tongue depressor
- Petroleum jelly
- Safety pins
- Hand cleansing agent
- Sunscreen
- Aspirin and non-aspirin pain reliever
- Cold pack
- Blanket
- Plastic bags
- Flashlight, flares and reflectors
- Activated charcoal
- Syrup of Ipecac
- Sting relief pad
- Alcohol swabs
- An up-to-date first-aid instruction card (or manual)

COLD WEATHER GEAR

And to be prepared for a cold weather emergency:

- Stock your vehicle with extra gloves, hats, blankets, a windshield scraper and thermal packs.
- Carry sand, salt or calcium chloride.
- If you don't have snow tires, carry tire chains. (Practice putting on the tire chains so you know how to use them.)

PART II

THE SCIENCE AND TECHNIQUES OF EVERYDAY DRIVING

Most drivers never think of car control until an emergency occurs. When the emergency does occur, it's too late to think about it. To control a car as efficiently and effectively as possible, you must understand some of the science — *as well as* the techniques — of driving.

This Part looks in detail at the control maneuvers you can make with a car — accelerating, steering, braking. It covers the basic science behind these maneuvers and discusses specific techniques you can use to maintain maximum control of your vehicle.

It also points out — perhaps more importantly — what can happen if you *lose* control by not accelerating, steering, or braking *properly* — and WHY. And it tells you how to *regain* control if you lose it.

Chapter 12

Introduction to Vehicle Dynamics:

The Physical Basis of Car Control

When you are driving a vehicle, you can do just two things: change speed and change direction. And you do these through the car's controls — the gas pedal, the brake pedal, and the steering wheel. But you don't just *use* these "controls" — in essence, you have to "control the controls" as the vehicle encounters various and ever-changing conditions in the driving environment.

Cars don't lose control all by themselves — except in the rare occurrence of an outright mechanical failure. It is vastly more likely for the *driver* to lose control of the car.

Cars can be compared to computers. A computer is an inanimate object until someone programs it. In the same way, a car is an inanimate object until someone drives it. We frequently talk about cars and computers in much the same way. We say "the computer said such-and-such..." or "the computer made a mistake." Which is nonsense. Computers don't make mistakes; they either work or they don't. The "mistake" is made by the computer's operator. Claiming that a car "lost control" is like saying the computer made a mistake.

Loss of Control — Two Types

There are two basic kinds of loss of car control.

- The first isn't so much a control loss as it is just plain **sloppy driving habits.** All of us are guilty of sloppy driving from time to time. Remember the time you were trying to pull out of a driveway and ran over the curb? Or that time you didn't see the car that was pulling out of the parking spot and nearly hit it?

This type of loss of control really means that, although you were sitting behind the wheel, you were basically along for the ride. Loss of concentration and not paying attention resulted in the fact that you weren't a driver — **you were a passenger who just happened to be sitting behind the wheel.** This is a very dangerous place for a passenger to sit!

- **The second type of control loss is a perfect expression of the term "loss of control."** Only it is not so much the *car* that is out of control as the *driver is* out of control. In this sense, "out of control" means everything you would imagine it to be: heart pounding, eyes bulging, palms and forehead sweating, mouth going dry, stomach in a knot, and one central thought — *"Oh my God, I'm going to die!"* — occupying center stage in your mind. At this point **you have absolutely no control of either yourself or the car,** and the vehicle is going wherever the laws of physics take it. This is truly "out of control."

Wherever the Laws of Physics Take It ...

Anyone who spends time behind the wheel of a car needs to understand what is takes for a car to go *out* of control. To do this, you must have a basic understanding of vehicle dynamics.

Don't let the term "vehicle dynamics" scare you off. It's nothing more than a term for the physical forces acting on the vehicle — physical forces that affect the driver's ability to change a car's speed and/or direction.

- **Each vehicle is designed with (force) "control limits"** *specific* **to the vehicle** — a Hummer, for example, handles forces differently than a VW Beetle.

- **If the driver takes action** (through the car's accelerating, braking, or steering controls) **that exceed these limits,** the driver will be unable to control the vehicle.

In other words, you have to understand **the capabilities of your vehicle,** and exactly what happens when *you move the vehicle's controls.* It's very simple.

And to understand *this,* it is vital that you understand the various physical forces that act on the vehicle.

These forces include:

- **Friction** created between the tires and the road.

- **Momentum** built up in the vehicle while underway.

- **Centrifugal forces** placed on the car when its path is altered while underway.

In the next several chapters we will explain how these forces are created as you:

- **Go** (change speed)

- **Stop** (change speed)

- **Turn** (change direction)

by controlling a car's four modes of operation:

1. **Forward travel at a steady speed** (mode)
2. **Accelerating** (mode)
3. **Turning** (mode)
4. **Braking** (mode)

And, you'll see that **you rarely operate a vehicle in one mode in isolation.**

- You may travel forward at a steady speed, but you'll probably turn a corner or curve, or change lanes at least sometime while doing so.

- Or you may accelerate while cornering.

- And you may have to slow down while you're traveling or turning, so you'll be braking some, too.

IN THE NEXT SEVERAL CHAPTERS, you'll not only see **how all these forces are interconnected as you drive,** you'll learn **specific techniques for controlling your vehicle in each mode.**

Chapter 13

Maintaining Traction:

Tire-to-Road Grip and Weight Transfer

The most important concept to understand in vehicle dynamics is that for a car to perform the four modes of operation (forward travel at a steady speed, accelerating, turning, braking), it must rely on **adhesion between the tire and the roadway.**

Tire Adhesion — Tire-to-Road Grip

Automobiles are supported by a cushion of air contained in four flexible rubber tires. If you could place a car on a glass floor and look at it from below, you would see *four patches of rubber, each a little smaller than a hand,* touching the glass. These are **the only points of contact between your vehicle and the road.** (See Figure 13-1, p. 116.) Each of these four small patches of rubber is known as a "contact patch" and these four tire patches create the traction that makes the car go, stop, and turn. (They are also the sources of the control feedback you receive from the car. See "Car Feel," p. 122)

The "limit of adhesion"

The maximum control capacity of the tire patches is called the "limit of adhesion." This limit is the maximum performance available from a *particular vehicle and tire design.* The "limit of adhesion" is determined by the **grip of the tires to the road**, which in turn is determined by:

1. The vertical force placed on the tire.
2. Tire design.
3. Condition and type of road surface.
4. Vehicle speed

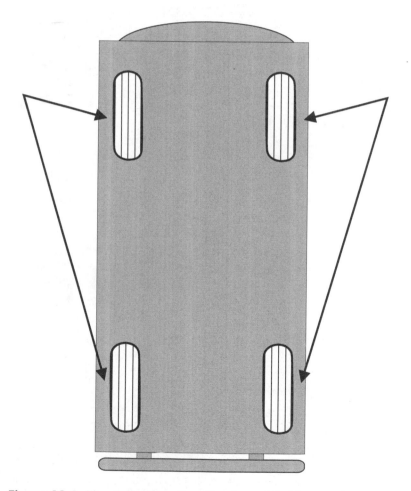

Figure 13-1. Tire Adhesion: Four Patches of Rubber. Each patch is a little smaller than a hand. The tire patches are the only points of control between your vehicle and the road.

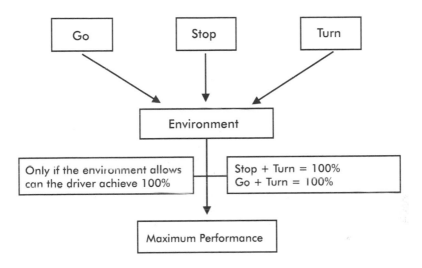

Figure 13-2. Maximum Performance Available from a Vehicle

5. Amount of turning force.

> **The maximum amount of acceleration, braking, and cornering (steering) forces possible with a given set of tires are all determined by this tire-to-road grip.**

Although there is a limit to what a car and its given set of tires can do, we sometimes force a car to *exceed* those limits — by over accelerating, over-steering, over-braking. And, if you *do* try to force a car to go beyond those limits — especially beyond the "limit of adhesion" — you will go out of control.

Maximum tire patch capability for performing a given action

The four tire patches enable the car to go, or stop, or turn. In motion, tire patches have a given amount of capability for performing a given action, such as stopping. If that capability is used up in a given action, then the patch cannot do anything else. (See Figure 13-2, p. 117)

- There can only be 100% performance from the vehicle if the environment allows it.

- If the driver uses 100% to stop, the car will not turn.

- If the driver uses 100% to turn, the car will not stop.

- If the driver uses 60% to stop, he can use 40% to turn.

- If the driver tries to use more than 100% by applying too much braking and too much steering, the driver will lose control of the vehicle.

- This all assumes that the environment allows the driver to use 100%. If the environment only allows 50%, then the driver will be able to use only 50% of the vehicle's capability.

Rolling Contact

To control a car, *rolling* contact between tires and the road surface must be maintained. If, for example, while you're driving along, something happens or something you do (accelerate, brake, turn) causes the tires to stop *rolling* and start *spinning without traction* or *sliding outright*, life gets exciting in a hurry.

If, for example, the tire patches on the two front tires (which are used to steer the car) stop rolling for any reason, you lose the ability to steer the car. Therefore, we are correct when we say:

- **The steering wheel does not steer or turn the car**; it merely **aims the front wheels.**

- **Rolling tires stop the car and turn the car.** Front tires must be rolling in order for the car to turn.

- To put it in simpler terms, **rolling friction is greater than sliding friction.**

- **Once the tires have stopped rolling** — and started sliding — **it is not possible to steer the car.**

Although it is important to understand what makes tires develop traction, it's far more important to understand what causes cars to *lose* traction and go out of control.

Weight Transfer to the Tire Patches

Weight transfer problems develop when a driver applies too much steering and braking force, or too much power and too much steering. The result in both cases is *excessive weight transfer to the tires,* which, in turn, puts too much pressure on the tire patches. **Too much weight on the tire patches causes the driver to lose control.**

- **Anytime you move a vehicle control** (gas pedal, brake pedal, or steering wheel), **you are transferring weight through the car's suspension system to the tire patches.**

- **If these forces produce stresses on the *tires* greater than they can accept,** those tires reach their limit of adhesion and let go. Again, the vehicle is out of control.

Referring to Figure 13-3, p. 120, you can easily see how weight transfers to the rear, front, left, or right depending on a driver's actions — and how excessive weight transfer can cause loss of control.

Weight transfer to the rear

The driver (Square 1) presses down on the gas pedal (Square 2). If we could put scales under the front and back wheels of the car when the gas pedal is depressed, we would see that the

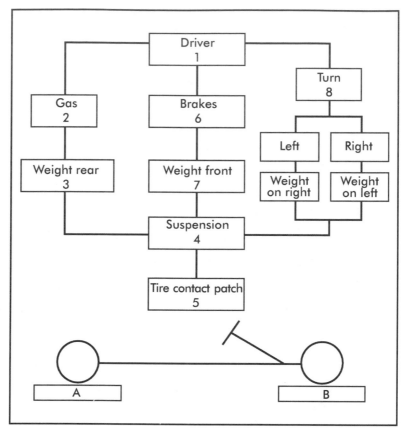

Figure 13-3. Block Diagram of Weight Transfer.

weight on the rear scale (A) increases and the weight on the front scale (B) decreases. In acceleration, weight was transferred from the front to the rear of the car (Square 3). This additional weight in the rear presses down on the car's suspension, affecting tire contact in the rear. If too much weight is applied, the rear tires will spin.

Weight transfer to the front

Once more, the car is on our imaginary scales. The driver (Square 1) applies the brake (Square 6), shifting weight onto the front end of the car (Square 7). This time, the front-end weight increases and the rear-end weight decreases. In this case, if too much weight is shifted forward, the front tires will lock up and steering control will be lost.

Weight transfer to the left or right

With the car under way, the driver turns the steering wheel (Square 8). If the wheel is moved to the right, weight is transferred to the left — once more, by way of the suspension and onto the tire contact patch.

Driving scenario — weight transfer in action

- You're driving your car, exiting a major highway, and **entering the off ramp at a speed of 25 mph.**

- Your car has **tires with a 1,500-lb adhesion limit.**

- **By turning onto the off ramp, you have placed 1,400 lbs. of force on your tires.** This is fine, the tires can handle this — unless, you have to apply the brakes or increase the angle of your turn. By doing either — or both — you will create more force on the tires, exceed their adhesion limits, and lose control of the car.

Remember: If your vehicle has tires capable of accepting 1,500 lbs. of vertical load, it can accept that load from braking, accelerating, or turning. It can take 1,500 lbs. and no more.

If you use all 1,500 lbs. accelerating, then try to turn or brake, you will reach the tires' adhesion limit and the tires will let go their grip on the pavement and you will lose control.

> **It is vital to understand the interrelationships among acceleration, braking, and cornering (steering) forces. The ways in which they *interact* is one of the most important concepts in driving.**

- **The amount you can move the steering wheel before losing adhesion** is determined by how hard you have applied the **brakes** at the time.

- The opposite is also true; **the amount of brakes you can apply** is determined by how much **steering force** has been applied.

> **In later chapters we will discuss how to drive yourself out of trouble, concentrating on the fact that the foundation of trouble-free driving is the relationship between the forces of stopping, accelerating, and turning as represented by the brake and gas pedals and the steering wheel.**

"Car Feel" — Keeping in Touch with the Control Limits of the Car

The characteristics of weight transfer onto the suspension and how those transfers affect the limit of adhesion is a major determining factor in just how the car *feels* to the driver. And it's not only possible but *desirable* to feel the control limits of a car long before those limits are *exceeded*.

> **Feeling the limits is mandatory because they permit careful drivers more control and give them a better idea of what is happening in the vehicle around them.**

But, **today many people feel that driving a car should feel like sitting on their living room sofa.** Operating their car's controls should not disturb their comfort in any way.

The people who feel this way buy the vast majority of the cars built every year in this country, so automobile manufacturers go to great lengths to abolish car "feel." **The end product is a car for people who are missing nearly all of the experience of driving.**

Most of us tend to be irrationally attached to certain makes of cars. Some of us come from families in which *everyone* owns and drives Chevrolets, others were raised in families where Ford may be the "officially sanctioned" car. We feel that some makes of cars are *intrinsically* better than others. But if we take a moment to think about these preferences from a rational point of view, the fact emerges that a car is simply a piece of machinery and nothing more. **And how that machinery communicates to you in terms of control — not just in comfort or aesthetics — should be taken into consideration.**

> **Cars communicate to their drivers in two basic ways: ride and handling. These are two very distinct sensations that are often confused with each other.**

Ride

Ride is the vertical motion of the wheels and tires as they rise and fall over irregularities in the road surface. Auto design engineers try to dampen this motion as much as possible, isolating it from the car's frame through the use of shock absorbers and other attenuating devices.

Ride is a comfort factor, one that can be hard or soft. A soft riding car smooths out the bumps on the road. A passenger could be drinking a cup of coffee as the car drove over a railroad crossing and not spill a drop. If a lot of the motion is felt in the car's body and passenger compartment, the result is a hard-riding and frequently uncomfortable car. In a hard-riding car, that same passenger would end up wearing that cup of coffee.

Many people mistakenly confuse ride with comfort — but, as we've said, ride is just one factor of comfort. A car that smooths out all the bumps of the road may be very *comfortable*, but may not necessarily be a good car for all *drivers*.

Handling

What is *handling*? Handling is the car's ability to remain in control when cornering or being driven through evasive maneuvers — that is, **it's ability to handle various weight transfers.**

It is also a complicated quality involving the entire driving system. **Handling depends on the machine and the environment, centering on the fact that a car is, at all times, a compromise between many factors.** While it is hard to define handling precisely, it is easy to make qualitative judgments as to what is good handling and what is bad.

In a study conducted by West German automaker Daimler Benz, researchers evaluated the current state of automotive handling technology. They came up with a compromise judgment as to **just what can be regarded as satisfactory handling qualities.**

- First, **the vehicle should respond quickly, but not skittishly or in a nervous way to control inputs.** Small movements of the wheel should not produce disproportionately large movements of the car. This response should be largely independent of vehicle speed.

- Secondly, **the vehicle should follow normal steering inputs correctly and without need of further correction.** Additionally, it should be possible for large lateral(sideways) movements of the car to be corrected with uncomplicated steering motions.

- Thirdly, **alternating quick releases of throttle and subsequent braking should produce no unexpected and/or dangerous side movements of the car.**

- Finally, **under varying road irregularities between the left and right sides of the car,** and in crosswind conditions, the driver **must be able to maintain a straight course easily.**

IN THE NEXT CHAPTER, we discuss what happens when the traction/weight transfer equation goes out of balance — and what you can do to regain control of your vehicle.

Chapter 14

Losing and Regaining Traction:

How to Handle Braking Skids, Power Skids, and Cornering Skids

As you have learned in the previous chapter, loss of tire adhesion (skids) is caused when a driver applies more input to the car than the design can take. Of course, the amount of input a given design can handle is affected by the weather, road conditions, and other environmental factors, but essentially, it is the driver who goofs by applying **too much input on the brakes, the accelerator, or steering wheel.**

> **When you lose control of the car, you have entered a skid situation — and *not all skids are created equal*. Skids have their own characteristics.**

Braking Skids

Fortunately, braking skids are less of a problem as more and more passenger cars come off the assembly line equipped with anti-lock (ABS) brakes and/or traction control mechanisms. (Most commercial vehicles have no ABS or traction control.)

> **Even if your own vehicle is equipped with all the bells and whistles the auto manufacturers offer, there is always the possibility of rentals being ill-equipped — so you should know how to handle braking skids with both ABS and non-ABS. (See Ch. 19, *Braking Control, Part II: Non-ABS and ABS Techniques*.)**

Front-wheel braking skid

In a front wheel braking skid severe enough to stop the forward wheels (usually caused by a hard brake application), the driver may suddenly find that steering the car has become impossible. No matter how much the steering wheel is turned, the car continues in a straight line ahead.

All the available friction capability of the front tires is being used by trying to stop. No turning, or "cornering" force, as it's known, can develop at the front wheels. If all the tire patches' friction capability is used trying to stop, then it becomes impossible to steer the car. The reason the car continues in a roughly straight line is due, in part, to simple physics (moving objects tend to take a straight path unless another force is exerted on them), and also the fact that the rear wheels, which continue to roll even though the front wheels are locked up, act as a sort of "rudder," keeping the car traveling forward.

Paradoxically, a front-wheel braking skid almost always creates the situation that drivers try hardest to avoid. Drivers slam on their brakes to stop, only to find themselves skidding right into what they were trying to avoid.

How do you control such a skid in a non-ABS car?

- **Get off the brakes,** which allows the front tires to start rolling again, and, above all, *keep the front wheels pointed straight.*

- **If you have moved the steering wheel sharply to the left** while skidding, and *then* release the brakes; *the car will turn sharply and violently in that direction.*

Rear-Wheel Braking Skid

What happens if the rear wheels stop rolling and lock up? **With rear wheels locked, the car reacts violently to the slightest movement of the steering wheel,** producing the maneuver known as **"spinning out."**

How do you avoid this?

- **Stay off both the accelerator and the brake** while regaining control by means of a technique known as "countersteering," or **turning the wheel in the same direction the rear end of the car swings.**

- Since the rear end may tend to "fish-tail," or swing back and forth, **it may be necessary to change the direction of the wheel several times before regaining control.**

- Throughout this procedure, keep in mind that **the general idea is to keep the nose in front of the skidding wheels at all times.**

Four-wheel braking skid

This is the type of skid that results when the driver tries to shove the brake pedal through the floorboards.

Unless you have Anti-Lock (ABS) brakes (see p. 182), this unusually hard application of the brakes locks up those wheels, which cease to rotate. In such a skid, the path of the car will not be predictable. There's just no way of predicting where the car is going.

Unfortunately, many drivers in a four-wheel braking skid don't immediately think they're in this kind of skid because they don't feel they hit the brakes hard enough to produce a skid.

There's only one solution to this problem: You must get those wheels rolling again. (See Ch. 19, *Braking Control, Part II: Non-ABS and ABS Braking Techniques* for in-depth discussion.)

- **If you *do not* have anti-lock brakes,** take your foot off the brake pedal — *now!*

Once the front tires are rolling, control is returned to the driver, who may then be able to steer out of trouble.

- **If you *have* anti-lock brakes,** maintain pressure and continue steering in the direction you want to go.

- **If the present danger requires some additional braking,** this must be done *gently,* with less pressure than before, or this whole dangerous chain of events will repeat itself.

Power (Acceleration) Skids

Excessive acceleration causes what is known as a power skid. Most power skids happen when roads are slippery.

Rear-wheel drive power skid

Power skids occur almost exclusively on rear-wheel drive cars. They're caused by too much power going to the rear wheels. The tire/road combination cannot accept that much power and the tire begins to spin. In a rear-wheel drive power skid, the back end of the car will swing out — in some instances spinning the car in a complete 360-degree spin.

This maneuver is probably familiar to anyone who has ever driven on ice.

- The solution to the rear-wheel power skid is to **ease your foot off the accelerator until the wheels stop spinning.**

- Then, and only then, **make any necessary steering corrections.**

Front-wheel drive power skid

Since front-wheel drive means the front wheels are the pair accepting power from the engine, in a front-wheel drive power skid, those are the wheels that are spinning. And, once again, this type of skid generally takes place on slippery surfaces.

- The best way out of a front-wheel drive power skid is to **take your foot off the gas** and **try to steer out of the skid without using the brakes.**

- If needed, **apply the brakes *very sparingly*.**

Cornering Skid

A cornering skid takes place when a driver enters a turn too fast and too sharply. This causes the rear end of the car to swing out.

- The best thing to do in this situation is **ease off the gas** and **avoid braking.**

- When you ease off, you'll find **the car's rear end will begin to track in its original position again.**

> **See Ch. 26, *Foul Weather Driving* for discussions on skidding and various weather/road conditions.**

IN THE NEXT CHAPTER, we discuss the science behind steering maneuvers — and how speed and tire adhesion enter into the steering control equation.

Chapter 15

Steering and G-Forces:
Vehicle Dynamics in Action

Newton's Laws of Motion Applied to Driving — Simplified

Sir Isaac Newton formulated several Laws of Motion that we can apply to driving. Basically the laws say that:

- **An object at rest tends to remain at rest** — *unless* you apply a force to it.

- **An object in motion tends to continue moving in a straight line at constant speed** — *unless* you apply force to it — which will either change its speed or direction, or both.

Applied to driving, we could say that if you step on the gas pedal (and your steering wheel is straight), you apply the force that will get the car moving — moving in a straight line.

And, if, while the car is in motion, you move the steering wheel to maneuver around a corner, or to avoid an obstacle, the car *tries* to follow a path dictated by the direction of the front wheels.

However, by turning the steering wheel while the car is moving, you also create *another* force that pushes on the car sideways, forcing it *away* from the desired direction of travel. The amount of this force depends on how *fast* you are going, how *sharp* you turn the steering wheel, and how *much* your vehicle weighs.

And, in order for the car *not* to be pushed sideways, the four tire patches on your car that are gripping the road must be able to "***push back***" with a force *equal* to the force generated by making the turn.

Your Vehicle's Control Limits

The forces we are talking about are called G (gravitational) forces and centrifugal forces — and **each vehicle is designed to withstand — or absorb — only so much of these forces before it becomes unstable.**

Box 15-1. **G-Force Ratings of Popular Car Models**

Various cars are designed to absorb a certain amount of G force. The amount of G force exerted on a car is a function of both the degree of sharpness of the turn and the speed at which the car is traveling during the turn. If this G force limit is exceeded, the result is loss of control.

If you're interested in how many Gs various car designs can take, pick up some of the automotive magazines available on any news stand. In them, you'll find reviews of various cars that include road tests and the G-force ratings that resulted from those tests.

Here are a few of the maximum G-force ratings of some of the cars we know and love:

Chevrolet Corvette	0.892 Gs
BMW 745i	0.87Gs
Cadillac Escalade	0.73Gs

Remember: A car is merely a machine; if we try to use that machine in such a way that its design limits are exceeded, then this machine, like any other, will not work.

So it is important for you to not only understand how the various *combinations* of your vehicle's speed and weight and the sharpness of your turns of the steering wheel can develop forces that affect your ability to control your car in any given situation, you must also understand **the control *limits* that are designed into your particular vehicle.**

To do this, you have to follow a two-step process:

- First you have to **figure out the G-force that is created by your handling of the vehicle** — how much you step on the gas pedal and how sharply you turn the steering wheel.

- Then you have to **compare the amount of Gs generated with the amount of Gs your vehicle was designed to absorb** (it's G rating) before it would become unstable — and you'd lose control.

Understanding these forces and control limits should give you an *intuitive* understanding of how you can better handle your vehicle.

In the next section, we introduce the Driving Equation and show you step-by-step how to use it to figure out the G forces created in a given situation — and how to interpret them in terms of control.

A WORD ABOUT EQUATIONS. Equations are engineers' ways of confusing us mortals. They are also a useful shorthand way of expressing complicated concepts. It's not as important for you to profoundly understand the equation as it is for you to intuitively know its consequences — that is, understand what you can do as a driver to overcome the effects of these forces and stay in control of your vehicle.

THE "DRIVING EQUATION" — FIGURING OUT THE G-FORCE

To figure out the G-force we use the following equation (the "Driving Equation")

$$LA = V^2 / R15$$

First, let's review the equation:

LA - This is lateral acceleration; the amount of G force exerted on the car. This is what we're trying to figure out.

V - This is how fast the car is traveling in miles per hour.

R - This is the radius of the turn, roughly equivalent to the degree of sharpness of the turn, or the amount the steering wheel is turned.

15 - This is the force of gravity (this is a constant).

WHAT THIS EQUATION IS SAYING is that the amount of force imparted to the car is determined by how fast we're driving and how sharp we'd like to turn, which is another way of saying how much we move the wheel.

Let's take an example and plug the figures into the equation:

Let's make a turn at an average street corner which has a 55-ft radius. We'll take that corner at a speed no one would think unreasonable, say, 20 mph. So for our equation:

V = 20 mph

R = 55 ft

The driving equation **LA = V^2 / R15 in this scenario thus becomes:**

$$LA = \frac{(20)^2}{(55)\,(15)} = \frac{400}{825}$$

So, LA — or the G-Force = **.49Gs**

If you compare this G force (.49) with the G-Force rating of your vehicle (let's say it's 0.8Gs), you'd be in fat city going around that corner with no control problems. If you exceed your vehicle's G-rating, however, you'd be in trouble.

You can further see this if you take the car's weight into consideration. If you multiply the weight of the car by the Gs in the scenario, you can figure out how many pounds of force are pushing the car sideways away from its desired path.

Let's follow the same example, figuring in the car's weight.

If the car, let's say, was a sedan that weighed 4,000 lbs., you'd multiply the G-force from our scenario (.49Gs) times the weight of the car (4,000 lbs.).

.49Gs x 4,000 lbs. = 1,960 lbs.

So 1,960 lbs. of sideways G-force on a 4,000 lbs. car would not throw it out of control.

How many pounds of sideways G-force *could* your 4,000-lb car with a G-rating of 0.8G absorb before becoming unstable? Simple. Multiply the weight of the vehicle times the G-rating:

4,000 lbs. x 0.8G = 3,200 lbs.

Your vehicle could absorb 3,200 lbs — and no more.

Remember: The lateral G-forces created in a turn is based upon both the vehicle's weight and the degree, or sharpness, of the turn.

- If we turned our 4,000 lb car in such a way that .7G was created, then we would have created 2,800 lb of force or 4,000 X .7 = 2,800 lb.

- If the car weighed *3,000* lbs. and was turned the same way, the equation would read 3,000 X .7 = 2,100, and so forth.

- And, if 4,000 lbs. of force are exerted on a 5,000-lb car, that's no big deal. But if you take a corner in such a way that 4,000 lbs. are being exerted on a 2,000-lb car, you're in big trouble.

So, what does all this mean in terms of what you as a driver have to do to maximize control while steering at speed? It means that you have to somehow control the Gs that your maneuvers create.

As we'll see in the next section, **a small change in G-force can make a very big difference in the way a vehicle handles.** And, if you study the Driving Equation, you can see that for the same scenario — same car (means same weight), and same corner (means same radius), **the only thing that can change the G-force results is your SPEED.**

Small Changes in Speed/Very Big Changes in G-Forces

Let's stick with our same example and run some different speeds through the equation.

If we double the speed to 40 mph, will there be twice as much force exerted on the car? Plugging those numbers into the equation gives us:

V = 40 mph or 58.8 ft/sec

R = 55 ft

LA = V2 / R 15 = (40)2 = 1600/(55)(15) = 1.94gS

If we multiply the weight of the car by the Gs we get:

4,000 lbs. x 1.95Gs = **7,808 lbs. of force**

In other words, with the same 4,000-lb car going around the same 55 ft corner, we have increased the amount of lateral force to 7,808lbs. — or approximately *four times the force encountered at 20 mph!*

It doesn't require a Ph.D. in mathematics to figure out that if you exert 7,808 lbs. of force on a 4,000 lb car, that force is more than sufficient to push that car into the *Twilight Zone*, or at least off the road.

This should be a startling observation! **Doubling the speed of a car doesn't double the force exerted on the car, it quadruples it** — because the force increases according to the *square* of the speed — the speed times itself.

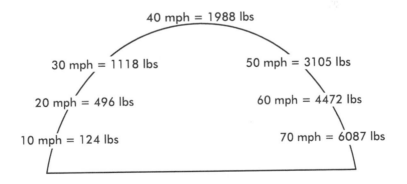

40 mph = 1988 lbs

30 mph = 1118 lbs   50 mph = 3105 lbs

20 mph = 496 lbs   60 mph = 4472 lbs

10 mph = 124 lbs   70 mph = 6087 lbs

Figure 15-1. Relationship of Speed to Lateral Acceleration. A 4,000-lb car turns the same corner at varying speeds. At 10 mph there is 124 lb of force on the car; at 40 mph there is 1,988 lb of force on the car.

So, in the equation, when you go from 20 mph to 40 mph it's really like going from 20 mph to 400 mph!

In other words, if a driver increased his speed by a factor of *two*, the amount of force exerted on the car goes up by a factor of *four*. Therefore, under the correct condition, **a small change in speed can easily produce far more force than the car was designed to accept** (see Figure 15-1, p. 139).

So what's the solution to maintaining control? (Drivers are always looking for magic answers to this one.) Guess what? *Don't drive too fast!*

> **According to the National Safety Council, 33.5 percent of fatal accidents are caused by excessive speed.**

THE TIRE ADHESION FACTOR

The Driving Equation has shown us how speed affects the maneuverability of a car when turning/steering — how speed, the sharpness of a turn, and the weight of the vehicle determine whether or not you might suffer an accident. **But there is another factor that comes into play, here, too** — the all-important **tire adhesion principle.**

- We have seen that when a driver moves the steering wheel to drive around a curve/corner, he creates a side force (lateral acceleration), pushing on the car's center of gravity.

- Let's say that in turning, the driver creates 3,000 lbs. of force pushing on the car.

- There must be a force of 3,000 lbs. pushing *back* on the car or the car will slide off the road.

- The resisting force is created by the tire contact patches. (*See p. 115*)

If, for example the turn produced 3,000 lbs. of force pushing on the center of gravity of the car, the tires at the front and rear of the vehicle *altogether* would have to push *back* with 3,000 lbs. of force. In this case, the car would be balanced and *wouldn't* slide off the road.

The scenarios in our Driving Equation examples indicate the effects of vehicle dynamics on cars whose tires are in optimum condition — that is, they can perform (grip the road) to the vehicle's intended performance standards.

But what happens if your tires are NOT in their best condition — they're not properly inflated and/or don't have at least the minimum tread depth — or you have mixed tire types on your vehicle (radials and bias-ply)? Even though you may be maneuvering your vehicle within the limits of its G-rating, and your speed is controlled, you may experience the phenomenon of understeer or oversteer when you attempt to control your vehicle through steering.

THE PHENOMENA OF UNDERSTEER AND OVERSTEER

Sometimes you'll be driving along and your car starts "talking" to you. Not like one of the modern, computerized cars that tell you to fasten your safety belt or that your windshield washer fluid level is low, but in the *seat of the pants* way with which pilots are familiar. **The car simply doesn't respond the way it should when you're steering. It seems to oversteer or understeer.**

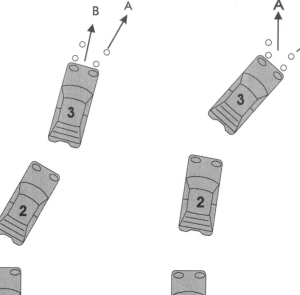

Figure 15-2. Understeer.
You aim at A, but arrive at
B

Figure 15-3. Oversteer.
You aim at A, but arrive at
B.

Neutral Steer, Understeer, Oversteer

In **neutral steer,** when the driver moves the steering wheel to negotiate a corner, he aims at a point and the car arrives at that point.

In **understeer** and **oversteer**, the driver moves the wheel to allow the car to enter the corner. He aims the car at Point A. But instead of arriving at Point A, the car goes to Point B — too far to the left in understeer (see Figure 15-2, above) and too far to the right in oversteer (see Figure 15-3, above). In both cases the car *fish-tails* in a see-saw motion.

The Physical Dynamics of Understeer and Oversteer

In a nutshell, understeer and oversteer are the interrelationship of the front and rear ends of the car. Let's take the same scenario we looked at in discussing tire adhesion a moment ago:

- The driver steered around a curve and created 3,000 lbs. of force pushing on the center of gravity of the car.

- To keep the car from sliding off the road, there must be a force of 3,000 lbs. of resisting force generated by the tire contact patches pushing back.

- Ideally the tires at front and rear of the vehicle would be pushing back with 1,500 lbs. from the front set and 1,500 lbs from the back set. The resisting force would be balanced.

In understeer, the *front* wheels have *less* traction than the rear. If, for some reason, the front tires can only provide 1,200 lbs. worth of resisting force (traction) and the rear tires provide 1,500 lbs., the result will be a sensation that suggests the front end of the car is going too far to the *left* from where the driver would like it to go.

In oversteer, it's the *rear* tires that are providing the lighter amount of traction, and the front tires that are loaded so that they adhere to the pavement better. The result is that the rear end of the car loses traction first, so that the rear begins to move toward the *outside* of the turn. This fish-tail effect may be encountered during a sudden application or withdrawal of *power* during a turn, or by a sudden movement of the *steering wheel* during a turn.

(The above is a bit of an over-simplification of what actually takes place, but only because it's rather complicated to explain the specifics of the vehicle dynamics involved.)

Causes of Understeer and Oversteer

The causes of understeer and oversteer are related to the condition and type of the tires on the vehicle — and the vehicle design.

Tire condition and type

- **Low tire pressure**

    Low *front* tire pressure (understeer)

    Low *rear* tire pressure (oversteer)

- **Uneven tire pressure**

    Uneven *front* tire pressure (understeer)

    Uneven *rear* tire pressure (oversteer)

- Sometimes a car will **understeer or oversteer in one direction and not in another.** This is due to the fact that **one tire has lower pressure than the other.**

    On the *front* (understeer)

    On the *back* (oversteer)

- **Bald tires**

    In the *front* (understeer)

    In the *back* (oversteer)

- **Mismatched tires.** In understeer this involves radials in the back and bias-ply tires on the front. The front of the car will push out, that is, resist the turn.

> **CAUTION: A quick shift from understeer to oversteer is very dangerous. If a car does this, check for tire inter-mix, the mismatching of bias-ply tires and radials in the same car. Cars must have one or the other type of tire *on all four wheels.***

Vehicle design and understeer

It is interesting to note that most automobiles built in the U.S. are designed to *produce* understeer.

In a study conducted by the Society of Automotive Engineers, results indicated that as the tendency for an automobile design to understeer increases, the accident rate decreases.

A reason for this may be that a car with a high value of initial understeer will tend to wander when traveling down a straight road and be relatively insensitive to minor steering inputs. This handling quality could be important in situations in which the driver's attention is momentarily distracted from the road. *So* American engineers feel it's safer for a car to have a degree of understeer built in.

How to Compensate for Understeer and Oversteer

To overcome understeer:

- Your objective should be to **get some of the vehicle's weight onto the front tires.** This will make the front tires grab the pavement more securely and start turning the vehicle.

- **Sometimes, just taking your foot off the gas** will transfer enough weight forward to do the job.

- In some cases, **it may be necessary to apply the brakes** in order to increase the weight transfer to the front wheels. If this is done, great care must be taken not to over-control the car and throw the vehicle into a state of *oversteer*.

To overcome oversteer:

- **Turn the front wheels to the outside of the turn.** That is, turn them in the direction the rear wheels are attempting to move.

- **Use the accelerator to apply power** so that power is applied to the rear wheels, which will force the car toward the inside of the turn and regain control. Applying power at this moment is tricky; too much power can spin the vehicle in the opposite direction.

Power Oversteer, and Trailing Throttle Oversteer

Power Oversteer

As you exit the corner you apply gas, and the back of the vehicle starts to swing out. The back of the vehicle is swinging out because you have applied too much gas and the back tires are loosing adhesion - to correct the problem you either have to steer less and give it less gas.

Trailing Throttle Oversteer

Also there is another form of oversteer that is called trailing throttle oversteer, which means that as you turn and take your foot off the gas the back of the car swings out. Trailing throttle oversteer is due to the back tires doing funky things when you transfer weight from the rear to the front. (Very common in armored vehicles). Correct trailing-throttle oversteer by smoothly increasing the throttle (to transfer weight to the rear tires) and apply steering to counter the rotation.

IN THE NEXT CHAPTER, we discuss the science and techniques for steering safety and effectively around curves and corners at speed.

Chapter 16

Curves and Cornering at Speed:

How to Handle the Road when It's <u>Not</u> Straight

In automobile Utopia, all the roads are the same width, all corners the same angle. The road surfaces are all the same, all uniformly wonderful and smooth as silk. There are no steep hills, no deep valleys, and drivers seldom have to even move the steering wheel because the roads are so incredibly straight.

Unfortunately, this automotive paradise rarely exists and we do need to do things like move steering wheels, and brake and

Figure 16-1. A Little Stretch of Road Utopia.
Scenic Route, New York State © Jon Huber 2007

accelerate. And, we have to drive around curves and corners —
whether we're driving just around town or around the country.

THE THREE TYPES OF CORNERS (CURVES)

**As far as drivers are concerned, there are three
types of corners:** constant radius, decreasing radius and
increasing radius corners. (See Figure 16-2, below.)

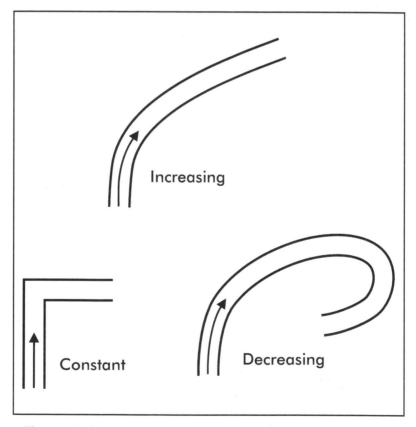

**Figure 16-2. Increasing, Decreasing, and Constant Radius
Corners.**

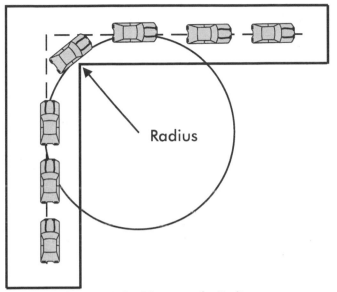

Figure 16-3. Diagram of a Radius.

- A **_constant radius_ corner** has a radius or "distance from a center line or point to an axis of rotation" (as the dictionary puts it) that is constant.

    A constant radius corner would become a circle if permitted to continue a full 360 degrees around.

- A **_decreasing radius_ corner** is a curve in which the turn angle becomes sharper as you drive around it. (See Figure 16-2, p. 148)

    A good example of a decreasing radius corner can be found on highway underpasses, in which an exit ramp curves around and under the highway.

- An **_increasing radius_ corner** requires a sharp turning angle at first, and then gradually straightens. (See Figure 16-2, p. 148)

    Some freeway access ramps are like this, beginning with a sharp turn required to get off the surface street and onto the freeway, then gradually straightening to allow traffic to speed up and enter the freeway traffic flow smoothly.

Knowing the various corner/curve types is very important, because they all require different types of driving.

THE SCIENCE OF HANDLING THE CURVES

Thousands of people are killed each year in collisions between vehicles, but more are killed in one-vehicle accidents. A driver loses control of her vehicle, skids off the road and careens into a telephone pole, or his vehicle turns over and over as it rolls down an embankment into a ditch. A curve is a likely place for this kind of accident.

As we covered in the previous chapter, there are two rules of physics about moving bodies that pertain to steering:

1. **Moving bodies tend to remain in motion.**

2. **Moving bodies tend to follow a straight path.**

To make a moving body follow a curved path, you have to use force to overcome its natural tendency to follow a straight one. A vehicle on a curve is a moving body with a natural tendency to go straight ahead. At each point on the curve the driver must use force — through steering — to keep the vehicle turning. The natural tendency to go straight ahead increases much more rapidly than the speed.

At 60 mph, there is *nine* times as much force on the vehicle than at 20 mph.

And as we covered in earlier chapters:

• **Effective steering depends on the traction between the road and the tires.** (Remember, traction refers to the tendency of the rubber of the tire to stick to the road instead of slipping and sliding over it.) (See Ch. 13, *Maintaining Traction*).

- **The part of a tire in contact with the road at any one time is about the size of the sole of a shoe.**

- **Four small patches of rubber are the only connection between the road and the vehicle.**

- **Anyone who has ever been in a skid knows that traction can be broken.** Whenever the tendency of the vehicle to travel in a straight line becomes too powerful for the traction holding the vehicle on the curve, the tires slide on the road and the vehicle starts to skid. (See Ch. 14, *Losing and Regaining Traction.*).

- **The force represented by the natural tendency of the vehicle to follow a straight line is opposed by the force you place on the car when you move the steering wheel.** These opposing forces can cause you to lose control of the vehicle.

 So control of the car while cornering is vital. As driver, your job is to drive as efficiently as possible, and to do this, you must overcome the tendency of the car to move to the *outside* of the turn.

CORNERING TECHNIQUES

Knowing how to maneuver around corners/curves is important for *all* drivers — whether you're an everyday motorist hoping for a smooth ride to work or uneventful Sunday afternoon spin, or an emergency worker who must drive through corners as quickly as possible.

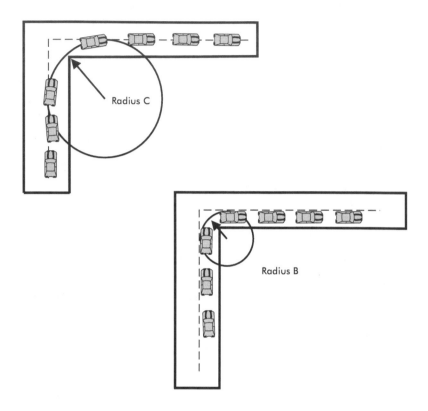

Figure 16-4. Big Radius vs Small Radius Corners. A car can be driven faster around radius C than it can around radius B.

The term used in driving schools for this move is "fast through the corner." But this doesn't mean how fast you are driving when you *enter* the corner/curve. Anyone can approach and enter a corner going fast — even too fast. "Fast through the corner" means to safely drive through a corner as quickly and efficiently as possible with skill and precision. In order to do this, drivers need only put as little steering force as possible on the car. And to do *this*, you "straighten out the corners."

"Straightening Out the Corners"

To drive a corner quickly and efficiently, you'll have to "straighten out the corner" or, in other words, make the path of the car through the corner the biggest radius possible. (See Figure 16-4 above.)

> **Remember (see Ch. 15, Steering and G-Forces) that in the Driving Equation (LA = V^2/R32.2), the letter R represents the radius of the corner. If the value for _R_ is big, it means the corner had a larger radius.**

A corner with the "biggest radius possible" means a corner not with a sharp turn, but with a gentle, gradual turn — one in which very little steering force is imparted on the car. Since the steering required is slight, the ride through the corner will be a comfortable one. What's more, the larger the corner's radius, the faster it can be driven through.

A corner's apex

There is an imaginary point on a corner or curve in the road called the "apex." This is the point at which the road begins to turn — which, depending on the dimensions of the curve itself, will be at some point on the curve's _inside_ path.

Outside-Inside-Outside Technique

In racing, this is called "taking a line." The line referred to is the path your car takes as it passes through the corner. Every corner in the world has a line and apex that allows a careful driver to maneuver through it as quickly and efficiently as possible.

The proper procedure for taking a corner at speed is to drive from the outside edge of the road as you enter the corner, then move to the inside to intersect the apex, and then back to the outside to exit the corner — all _without_ driving into the other lane of traffic.

1. **As you enter a corner, your car should be on the *outside* of the curve**, still in your assigned lane (see Figure 16-4, p. 152), of course, but to the *outside* of that lane.

Never drive in the oncoming lane, or a lane that rightfully belongs to another car — but do make good use of the entire road available to you.

---

2. **Entering the corner, gradually steer your car to the *inside* of the corner.** Your inside tire (the tire on

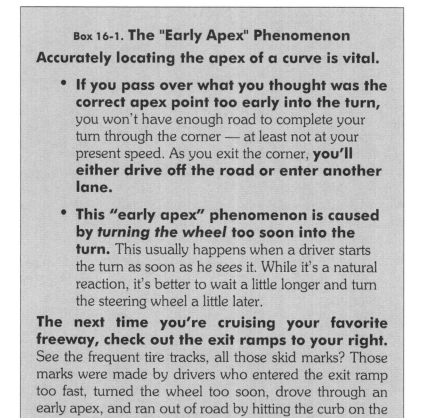

Box 16-1. **The "Early Apex" Phenomenon**

Accurately locating the apex of a curve is vital.

- **If you pass over what you thought was the correct apex point too early into the turn,** you won't have enough road to complete your turn through the corner — at least not at your present speed. As you exit the corner, **you'll either drive off the road or enter another lane.**

- **This "early apex" phenomenon is caused by *turning the wheel* too soon into the turn.** This usually happens when a driver starts the turn as soon as he *sees* it. While it's a natural reaction, it's better to wait a little longer and turn the steering wheel a little later.

The next time you're cruising your favorite freeway, check out the exit ramps to your right. See the frequent tire tracks, all those skid marks? Those marks were made by drivers who entered the exit ramp too fast, turned the wheel too soon, drove through an early apex, and ran out of road by hitting the curb on the outside. Their problem? Picking an early apex.

the side of the car in the direction you are turning) should ride over the "apex" — which, as we've said, depending on the dimensions of the curve itself, will be at some point on the curve's inside path. (See Box 16-1 below.)

3. **Once safely past the apex, the car will return to the outside of the road** pretty much all by itself.

Outside-inside-outside scenario

Let's take your **average run-of-the-mill 90-degree street corner, with the street 33 feet wide.** We'll drive through it two different ways and get some interesting results.

- **If we take the corner by hugging the inside of road,** we make a 50-ft. radius.

- But, **if we take the ideal line through this corner,** entering on the outside, covering the inside apex, and exiting on the outside, we have driven the largest radius possible: 138 ft.

If you wish, you can work out the mathematics of this maneuver with the equation

$$LA = V^2/R32.2$$

If you don't, it should be obvious that it is far easier and quicker to drive a corner with a 138-ft. radius, than a 50-ft. radius.

Speed and Braking While Cornering

You can take the best possible "line" through a corner, but if you take it with too much speed, you could still wind up off the road or into another lane — and suffer the consequences.

Approaching a corner very fast, only to have to slam on the brakes and crawl around the corner is inefficient, dangerous, and accomplishes nothing.

As you approach a corner, judge the speed at which you feel you can *safely* enter that corner.

- **Often corner and ramp speeds are posted** on highways.

- **Pick a speed a little lower than you feel the turn requires.** You are not a racing driver, trying to blow through the corner while setting a new world's record in the process. *Leave room for error.*

- **As you approach a curve, slow down enough** so that after you are in the curve, you can keep your engine pulling, maintain your speed, and then accelerate to leave the curve faster.

- **Do not wait until you are in the curve to apply your brakes.**

- **If you *must* apply your brakes in a curve,** be careful. Use a gentle pumping motion until you are sure it is safe to keep continuous pressure on the pedal.

Never enter a corner as fast as you can and hope that your brakes can slow you down sufficiently for you to survive this experience. If you've already used up your tires' capacity for stopping and then try to use them for control, you're in for a big, nasty, tire-screeching, fender-bending surprise.

- **Start turning your wheels** just *before* you reach the point at which the road begins to turn (the apex).

- **Once in a curve, stay on your own side of the road and stay as far over as you reasonably can.**

Do not try to make a curve easier by cutting across the lane of oncoming traffic.

- **Maintain a moderate speed** and the curve will be easy enough to handle on your side of the road.

A cornering skid

Remember from our discussion on *Losing and Regaining Traction* (Ch. 15), a cornering skid takes place when a driver enters a turn too fast and too sharply. This causes the rear end of the car to swing out.

- The best thing to do in this situation is **ease off the gas and avoid braking.**

- When you ease off, you'll find the car's rear end will begin to track in its original position again.

Remember, You Cannot Judge the Next Curve By the Last One

Roads with uniformly sharp or gentle curves are probably safer than roads with curves of varying degrees. But on most roads, curves vary a good deal. Assume that unfamiliar curves are *sharp.* You can always speed up if you are wrong, but you may not always be able to slow down.

IN THE NEXT CHAPTER, we look at how your speed affects the distance you need to stop safely — and how to determine and maintain safe following distances to give yourself an "out" should you have to brake suddenly in an emergency.

Chapter 17

Speed and Safe Stopping Distances:

The Time-Distance Relationship in Stopping and Turning

There are many occasions where we have to drive fast. **But how fast is fast enough, and how slow is too slow?**

Most of us would agree that 100 mph is fast and 20 mph is slow. But these are both relative values dependent on conditions. For anyone who has ever tried to drive on an icy road down an icy hill toward a busy intersection, 20 mph is downright *exciting*.

Speed Plays All Kinds of Tricks On Us

Among the most deadly lurk in the relationship of speeds to stopping distances. Table 17-1, p. 160 for example, shows that it takes 55 feet to stop a car on dry pavement at 30 mph.

If we double that speed, do we double the stopping distance? Sadly, no. In fact, the stopping distance increases by a factor of *four*. That's a good rule of thumb to remember.

> **For every doubling of the car's speed, it takes *four* times as much distance to bring the vehicle to a halt.**

Similarly, **if you drive from a dry surface onto a wet surface, the time needed for safe stops increases dramatically.** Why? Drivers will usually answer, "Because the road is slippery." But just what does that mean? It means the coefficient of friction between the road and tire is less than that needed for good, safe traction. (See Ch. 13, *Maintaining Traction*.)

Table 17-1. How Long Does It Take to Stop a Car?

mph	Dry(ft.)	Wet(ft.)	Snow(ft.)	Ice (ft.)
20	25	70	105	160
30	55	110	170	275
40	105	170	275	
50	188	250	410	
60	300	350		
70	455			

You must be aware of the effects of speed on braking distances. The faster you go, the longer it takes. Learn this intuitively, so you won't have to think about it — you'll just know it. Misjudging or disregarding speed can be a killer.

According to the National Safety Council, excessive speed is the single largest cause of accidents. This doesn't mean just driving over the speed limit. This means going too fast for the traffic situation developing around you, plain and simple.

Take a closer look at Table 17-1 above. Unless it's a real emergency, driving fast merely for the sake of driving fast is not too bright.

Miles Per Hour (mph) vs Feet Per Second (fps)

As a car is in motion down a road, the driver of that car is managing time and space (distance). As we drive, we measure time and space by using the car's speedometer. However, the speedometer is not the *best* reference possible for measuring time and space (or distance).

Speedometers indicate speed by measuring it in terms of *miles per hour* (mph) — a natural unit of reference that everyone is familiar with in driving discussions. But in terms of controlling a vehicle in split-second scenarios, mph is not a very useful unit of measure.

Consider: Accidents do not take *hours* to happen; they occur in *seconds*, even tenths of seconds. And they happen in very small physical areas, measurable in *feet* and sometimes inches, and certainly not in *miles.*

So, we need to rethink our frame of reference when we talk about controlling a car about how accidents happen. The frame of reference we'll find most valuable for this is feet per second (fps).

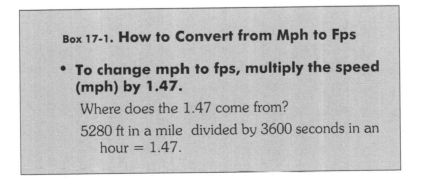

Table 17-2. Conversion from Miles Per Hour to Feet Per Second

Speed (mph)	Distance (ft./sec.)
20	29.4
30	44.1
40	58.8
50	73.5
60	88.2

Box 17-1. How to Convert from Mph to Fps

- **To change mph to fps, multiply the speed (mph) by 1.47.**

  Where does the 1.47 come from?

  5280 ft in a mile divided by 3600 seconds in an hour = 1.47.

Box 17-2. The *Easier* Way to Convert Mph to Fps

If you don't mind being off a bit in your calculations, or you're a driving instructor and would like to explain this concept to your students, but don't feel like multiplying by 1.47 every time you want to convert mph to fps, there is an easier way of doing all this.

- **First, round off 1.47 to 1.5.** That's a mathematically legal maneuver. The math cops won't write you a citation for doing that.

- **Now to change mph to fps, multiply by 1.5 instead of 1.47.**

- **You can do this easily by *adding*.**

> **Take *half* of the original mph and add it to the original mph.**

Say you're going 20 mph and want to know how much that is in fps.

> **Take *half* of 20 (which is 10) and *add* it to 20 (which will give you 30).**
> **(Half of 20 = 10, and 20 + 10 = 30).**

So if you were going 20 mph you would be moving at the rate of approximately 30 fps.

- **You can easily apply this to any mph conversion:**

Half of 20 mph is 10 — 20 + 10 = 30 ft/sec

Half of 30 mph is 15 — 30 + 15 = 45 ft/sec

Half of 40 mph is 20 — 40 + 20 = 60 ft/sec

Using feet per second as a measurement makes a big difference when discussing accident causes.

Time-Distance Driving Scenario

You're driving along at 40 mph (or 58.8 fps) . . .

- Something causes you to look away from the road for three seconds.

- At the same moment, another driver starts to cross an intersection 300 feet (the length of a football field) in front of you.

- Since your attention was diverted for three seconds and you were traveling at 58.8 fps, you drove a total 176.4 feet without looking where you were going (58.8 x 3 seconds = 176.4 ft).

- This puts you 123.6 feet from the intersection and its conflicting traffic.

- At this point, you look forward again, see the other traffic and realize you've got to do something.

- Can you avoid hitting that other car? Can you manage the remaining time and distance?

Let's examine this situation a little more closely.

- You're now 124 feet in front of the conflicting traffic, and closing with that traffic at 58.8 fps.

- If you can get your foot on the brake in a half of a second, you're very fast. Traveling at your speed, that half of a second represents about 30 feet. So at the point you start applying your brakes, you are about 92 feet from the traffic, still doing 40 mph (58.8 fps). Can you stop in time? Can you manage the distance?

- At this point, avoiding a collision would depend more on luck than skill. The problem here is excessive speed.

Time-distance-weight driving scenario

If you remember from Ch. 13 on the effects of weight transfer and tire traction (adhesion), you know that there is another factor that must be considered here as well. Let's see what happens when we factor weight into the situation when you have to make a sudden stop in a potential accident scenario.

- Your hypothetical car is equipped with tires capable of absorbing 1500 lbs. of vertical force. At this point, they will lose adhesion.

- Your speed is 30 mph, which multiplied by the conversion factor of 1.47, works out to 44 ft/sec.

- Your hypothetical day is a clear, sunny one, road conditions are excellent, our tires have a good grip on the road.

- Suddenly, a child on a bicycle appears 90 ft in front of you. It takes you half a second to get your foot to the brake pedal — meaning you have consumed 22 ft just getting your foot in position to apply the brakes. You now have 68 ft left before your car will strike the child.

- You panic and smash down hard on the brake.

- By doing so, you have transferred excess weight from the back end to the front end of the car. The weight transferred is more than the 1,500 lbs. the tires are designed to accept.

- This causes the front tires to slide, because they have passed their limit of adhesion. And since you use the front tires to steer, you've also lost directional control of the car.

- Therefore, sadly, you cannot steer away from the child.

Sadly, this mathematical scenario ends in hypothetical tragedy.

Time Needed to Cross an Intersection

According to an accident fact book prepared by the National Safety Council, 27.9 percent of all fatal urban traffic accidents occur at intersections. Another study, funded by the Federal government, indicates a higher incidence of intersection accidents — some 37 percent.

It's easy to misjudge the amount of time needed to cross an intersection. It takes about 4 seconds to cross a two-lane road safely.

If another car is approaching the intersection at 40 mph, and that car is 180 feet away (which translates to about three seconds away from you), and you choose that moment to cross the road, you're probably going to have an accident. Two objects cannot occupy the same space at the same time, at least not in this universe.

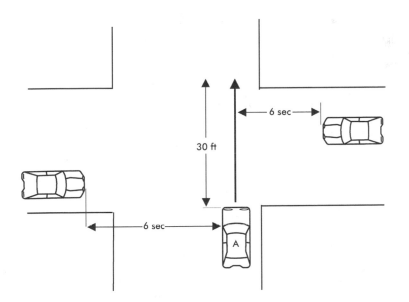

Figure 17-1. Time Needed to Cross an Intersection

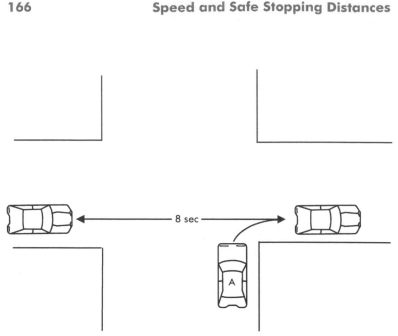

Figure 17-2. Time Needed to Make a Right Turn. From a stop, it takes six seconds to turn right and accelerate to 30mph. You should have at least eight seconds lead time before turning to the right.

Time Needed to Turn at an Intersection

Turns are also potential causes for disaster in intersections.

   If you want to turn right (see Figure 17-2 above):

   • From a stop, it takes six seconds to turn right and accelerate to 30mph.

   • Beginning such a turn, make sure that any vehicles approaching from the left are at least seven or eight (or even more) seconds away.

   If you want to make a left turn (See Figure 17-3, p. 167):

   • You'll need seven seconds to make the turn, attaining a top speed of 30 mph in that time.

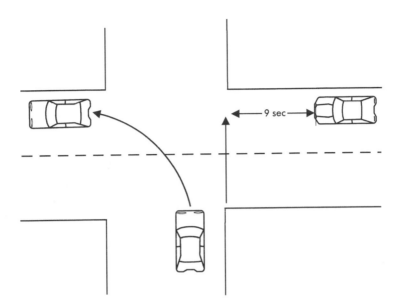

Figure17-3. Time Needed to Make a Left-Hand Turn. From a stop it takes seven seconds to turn left and accelerate to 30 mph. You should have at least nine seconds lead time before turning to the left.

- You should have at least nine seconds lead time before turning to the left.

   For example, if a car is approaching the intersection at 40 mph, and is 300 feet away, it will be at the intersection in about five seconds. For you, making a seven-second left-hand turn, this scenario spells collision.

Remember: **The left-hand turn requires *more* time because you are crossing one or more traffic lanes. The left-hand turn is more dangerous because in many situations it will put you into a conflicting path with oncoming cars — twice.**

SAFE FOLLOWING DISTANCES AND BRAKING

A great deal of the success of the various emergency-braking maneuvers depends on the driver's alertness and powers of observation. **To be a safe driver, you need space all around your vehicle.** When things go wrong, space gives you time to think and act. To have space available when something goes wrong, you need to *manage* space.

Of all the space around your vehicle, **the area ahead of the vehicle — the space you are driving *into* — is most important.** You need space ahead in case you must suddenly stop.

When driving, you should be looking ahead; indeed, **you should mentally be ahead of your car by at least six seconds.** At 30 mph, a six-second-eye lead means your eyes should be focused at least 285 ft in front of the car.

Sadly, **when driving in traffic, most untrained drivers are focused so closely they only react to the brake lights of the car in front of them.** When the driver in front of them hits the brakes, so do they. Sometimes they're too late. If you ask these brake-light followers why they persist in this strange habit, they'll invariable tell you, "I can't see around the car in front of me, so I have to react to that car's brake lights." These people don't realize that the reason they cannot see around the car in front of them is because they are following them *too closely*. If the vehicle they are following is a large one, such as a tractor-trailer, it only makes matters worse.

A Typical Following-Distance Scenario

Let's look at a scenario that happens every day.

- A motorist is driving at 30 mph and you are following him at the same speed, some 30 ft behind.

- Both cars approach an intersection and the light changes yellow. The motorist hits the brakes.

- It's a beautiful day in the neighborhood, so you are not as alert as you should be and you allow a whopping full second to pass before starting to react to the situation.

- Once the motorist applies the brakes, it will require about 55 ft to stop that 30 mph car.

- So now, a stopped car is 85 ft in front of you. If you are doing 30 mph, you are moving at 44ft/sec. Assuming a normal reaction time of .75 seconds, and adding the fact that your attention was diverted for one second, that means you will not get a foot to the brake pedal before having traveled 77 ft.

- If the front of the motorist's stopped car is 85 ft from you, and the car is 15 ft long, then its rear end is just 70 ft away from the your front end.

- Since it's going to take 77 ft before you get your foot to the brake, everyone involved is in for whole lot of hurting.

If the same example is re-examined and that one second of diverted attention is eliminated, an accident is *still* the outcome — even if you applied the brakes the instant you saw the motorist's brake lights come on. The rear end of that car is still 70 ft from your car's front end. How long does it take to stop at 30 mph? It takes 88 ft to come to a complete stop. That isn't enough and an accident is the result. The problem? You where following too closely.

> **ABS or non-ABS braking, throwing out an anchor, dragging your feet, all the fancy braking techniques in the world won't help if you follow other traffic too closely.**

So, our objective when it comes to following is simple: Keep a safe distance between you and the car ahead.

How Much Space *Should* You Keep in Front of You?

* One good rule is to keep **at least one second for each 10 feet of vehicle length at speeds *below* 40 mph.** For the average 20-foot car, this means if you're driving below 40 mph, you'd leave 2 seconds of space between you and the car ahead.

* **At greater speeds,** for safety, you must **add one second for every additional 10 mph.**

> **This becomes particularly important if you are driving a long vehicle — an RV or a truck, for example.**

* **If you are driving a 40-foot vehicle at a speed below 40 mph,** you should leave 4 seconds between you and the vehicle ahead.

  In **a 60-foot vehicle,** leave 6 seconds.

* **If you are driving that 40-foot vehicle faster than 40 mph,** you should leave 5 seconds between you and the vehicle ahead.

  In the **60-foot vehicle,** leave 7 seconds.

How Do You Figure Out How Much Space You Have?

1. **Pick a fixed object on the road** (a shadow on the road, a pavement marking, or some other clear landmark).

2. **When the car ahead of you passes the marking, count off the seconds** — one thousand and one, one thousand and two, and so on — **until you reach the same spot.**

3. **Compare your count with the rule of one second for every 10 feet of length.**

4. **If you pass it before the time is up,** you're driving too closely.

Safe Following Distances When Driving at Night

Remember that your vision is affected by the availability of light (see p. 20, *Seeing at Night*). Quite simply, you don't see as well at night as during the day — and this affects safe driving distances.

- At night, **you can only see safely as far as your headlights illuminate the road ahead** — 200 feet for low beams, 300 feet for high beams.

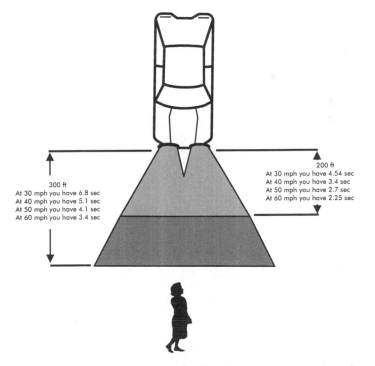

300 ft
At 30 mph you have 6.8 sec
At 40 mph you have 5.1 sec
At 50 mph you have 4.1 sec
At 60 mph you have 3.4 sec

200 ft
At 30 mph you have 4.54 sec
At 40 mph you have 3.4 sec
At 50 mph you have 2.7 sec
At 60 mph you have 2.25 sec

Figure 17-4. Night Vision vs Stopping Distances. Low beams illuminate the road ahead 200 feet. High beams 300 feet.

- Therefore, at night, when driving the average 20-foot car, make sure to **adjust the two-second rule for traffic ahead** of you to a **three-second rule.** When driving a longer vehicle, adjust accordingly (see p. 170. Don't overdrive your headlights. (See also Chapter 27, *Driving Safely at Night.*)

Specific Following Distances for Certain Vehicles

The rules for safe following distances differ for some vehicles — for example, **buses, trucks and fire engines.** You should know these rules — whether you are driving such a vehicle or just following behind it.

- When driving outside of cities and towns, a **bus or truck** should not travel closer than 200 feet behind another bus or truck.

- If you are behind **a fire engine when it is answering an alarm,** the minimum safe following distance is 500 feet. **Violators can be prosecuted.**

> After a little practice, you will know how far back you should drive. Also remember that when the road is slippery, you need *more* space to stop.

IN THE NEXT CHAPTER, we discuss the science of HOW a car stops when you step on the brake pedal.

Chapter 18

Braking Control, Part I

The Science of How a Car Stops

Brakes are by far the most important, most sensitive automobile control. Brakes are also the most challenging control to operate. And today they come in two flavors — ABS (Anti-locking Brake System) and non-ABS. While the techniques of braking differ between the two during *emergency* braking situations (see Ch. 19, *Braking Control, Part II: Non-ABS and ABS Braking Techniques*), the *science of braking in general* — the laws of physics — is the same for both.

Brakes Don't Stop Cars

Few drivers realize that brakes don't stop *cars*. Brakes stop *wheels* from rolling.

- **The friction of the tires against the road surface stops the car.** If brakes alone stopped cars, then cars would never skid.

- And the **maximum amount of friction** between tire and road **occurs just before the tire stops rolling.**

  The engineering explanation for this is that **rolling friction is greater than sliding friction**, or that a tire rolling across pavement has more stopping capability than a tire sliding across pavement.

Brake Pedal Pressure and Loss of Control

Although the concept of tire friction stopping a car is central to the whole dynamic of the moving vehicle, most of us who were

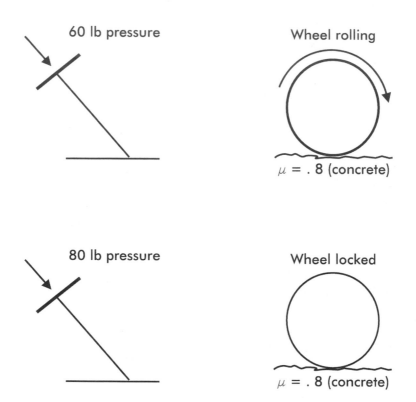

60 lb pressure

Wheel rolling

$\mu = .8$ (concrete)

80 lb pressure

Wheel locked

$\mu = .8$ (concrete)

Figure 18-1. Brake Pedal Pressure and Loss of Control.

taught to drive were taught that to stop the car, all we had to do was step on the brakes. **What most us weren't taught was that after a given point, pressing harder on the brake doesn't stop the car any quicker.** In fact, in a *non-ABS* vehicle, pressing too hard on the brake could get you into big trouble. Consider:

- The average male can step on the brake with 140 to 185 lbs of pressure. The average female can hit the brakes with between 70 to 100 lbs of pressure.

- In an emergency situation, if a driver applies 80 lbs of pressure to the brake pedal, and in so doing locks the wheels and stops the tires from rolling, that driver has actually created less friction between tire and road.

- If the brakes were applied with 60 lbs pressure, enough to slow the car but still allow the wheels to roll, the effect is to create *more* friction between tire and road.

- A locked-up, skidding wheel is experiencing a lower level of friction than a slowing, but still rotating, tire.

- With less friction, more time and distance are required to stop the car.

- The really bad thing that happens is that with the tires locked (not rolling), the driver has lost the ability to steer the car, and that can hurt.

> **At this point, in a non-ABS vehicle, applying more brake pressure will do nothing but make the situation worse.**

Here is where the confusion starts.

- **With an ABS vehicle, however**, you could press as hard as your foot can press and *good* things would happen. You'd still be able to steer the car — and if there is truck in front of you, that is a good thing.

The Vehicle Stopping Equation

When a vehicle is stopping or slowing down, it has to overcome the momentum that has been built up in the moving car. The following equation shows what's involved. You don't have to memorize the equation, but a quick examination of it can do much to help you understand why stopping a car in each circumstance is a completely unique situation. The equation is:

$$S=V^2/2 \; \mu g$$

S = Stopping

V = Velocity

μ = Coefficient of friction (pronounced MU)

G = Acceleration of gravity (32.2)

It's the combination of speed(s) and that little μ that can get us in a lot of trouble. From the equation, we can see that the *faster* we go the more distance is required for us to stop, and that the lower the value assigned to μ, the more distance required for us to stop.

What's especially disturbing is the fact that as speed is *doubled*, the distance required to safely stop is *quadrupled*.

For instance, if a car traveling at 20 mph is accelerated to 40 mph; its stopping distance does not increase by a factor of two, but by a factor of *four*.

Look what happens when we change the value for μ in the equation.

- **The value μ changes as the environment changes,** and when μ changes, the driving environment can get exciting in a hurry.

- For instance, if you are driving at 50 mph on a surface with a coefficient of friction (μ) of .8 (that of a dry concrete surface), it will require 104 ft to stop the car, not counting driver reaction time.

- If the same car is at 50 mph when it encounters a surface with a coefficient of friction (μ) of .05, the stopping distance increases to 1,888 ft., or a little more than a third of a mile.

> **Consider this equation a basic fact of life when it comes to stopping a car.**

- **The faster the car is traveling, the more distance it needs to stop.**

- Like centrifugal force, **speed and stopping distance are not linear.** Small changes in speed mean *big* changes in the distances required to safely stop.

- **If road conditions are slippery,** the coefficient of friction (or value μ of the equation above) decreases, and the required distance for a safe stop will increase *dramatically.*

- **Those who drive fast on a slippery road** will spend a great deal of time in the hospital and/or in court.

IN THE NEXT CHAPTER, we explain differences between Anti-Lock Brake System (ABS) and non-ABS — and detail the specific techniques for using both effectively and safely.

Chapter 19

Braking Control, Part II
Non-ABS and ABS Techniques

There are almost as many ways of braking a car to a stop as there are reasons for stopping. There is the gentle stop at a traffic light, and there is the *"Oh, my God!"* sort of life-and-death stop that nearly stops your heart as well as your car. Obviously, this latter type is most likely encountered in the emergency situation and is the one we're going to discuss here. And it is here where there is a huge difference between non-ABS and ABS-equipped vehicles.

> **Braking, you'll see, is not as easy or as simple as "press hard on the brake pedal."**

The Difference Between Non-ABS and ABS

ABS is an abbreviation for Anti-lock Braking System, and was developed to reduce skidding and maintain steering control in an *emergency* situation. During normal, non-emergency braking, ABS works the same as non-ABS. But when you have to brake *hard* in an emergency situation, ABS and non-ABS work differently, and each requires a different braking technique on the part of the driver. (The techniques for ABS and non-ABS braking will be covered separately later in the chapter.)

ABS is basically a conventional braking system that is helped by computer technology. During *hard* braking, sensors in each wheel let the computer know if all the wheels are turning at the same speed — or if one or more wheels is trying to stop rolling. If a wheel tries to stop rolling, a series of hydraulic valves limits or reduces the braking on that wheel. The computer in the vehicle essentially pumps the brakes for you in a special way — stopping the car as quickly as possible while preventing skidding and allowing you to have steering control. (Aren't computers great)? If you take your foot off the brake, however, it's like shutting off the computer — and that's not good.

Under normal conditions, the anti-lock system will *not* be activated. However, should the braking force exceed the available adhesion between the tires and the road surface, the system will *automatically* activate.

The bottom line with ABS brakes is that **under most conditions ABS brakes do not help you stop *quicker*.** Their life-saving ability is in helping you **maintain steering control** during braking so you can avoid what ever is in front of you.

> **The ABS is not a miracle worker, cannot repeal the laws of physics, and cannot make you immune to bad road conditions, or worse yet, bad judgment. It is still your responsibility to drive at reasonable speeds for weather and traffic conditions, and to always leave a margin of safety.**

NON-ABS BRAKING

An analysis of what happens in a non-ABS vehicle in emergency crash situations shows a very high likelihood of one or more of the vehicles being completely out of control. "Out of control" here means that just before the accident occurred, the vehicle was either spinning or skidding. In many of these situations, excessive braking was identified as the main culprit.

This news that improper braking can easily throw a car out of control comes as a revelation to most drivers, who associate loss of control with harsh or abrupt movements of the steering wheel.

Bear in mind just what loss of control really is. No control means that the driver is not, and cannot, predict the path the car will follow. The car moves as if it had a mind of its own, spinning, skidding, and sliding. Actually, the car is responding to the laws of physics and those of motion, but those responses can look pretty random to the innocent bystander.

Loss of control *frequently* occurs in emergency situations.

- We will assume, for purposes of discussion, that the driver's reaction to this control loss will be **hard, excessive braking.** In a non-ABS car, hard braking means the application of 50 to 100 lbs of pressure.

- **How hard *should* the brakes be applied in an emergency?** It's not easy to provide an answer that's correct for all situations, due to the many variables involved. The same amount of brake pressure that brings you to a safe and comfortable stop on a sunny, dry-pavement day probably won't work on a rain-soaked evening.

"Controlled Braking" in Non-ABS Vehicles

The braking method preferred by professional driving instructors is known as "controlled braking." This technique calls for pressure to be applied on the brake pedal almost up to the point of lock-up. All the while, the driver must be aware that the more brake pressure applied, the less steering leeway she'll have.

Let's take a step-by-step look, however, at a real-life scenario of the "controlled" braking process for a non-ABS vehicle:

1. The steering wheel is pointing the car's front wheels straight ahead.

2. The driver applies 50 lbs of pedal pressure.

3. The front wheels reach their point of optimal road friction — the point just before they lock and cease rolling.

4. Unfortunately, by this time there isn't enough room between the car and the obstacle that the driver is trying to avoid hitting. The driver sees a collision is quickly becoming unavoidable.

5. In a further effort to avoid the collision, the driver turns the wheel.

6. While the steering wheel is movable, a slight movement of that wheel will cause the front wheels to lock up, rendering steering completely ineffective.

So, while "controlled braking" works well in theory, we see that the theory has a way of being disproved in the real world. When driving, always bear in mind that a brain-boggling, panic-inducing *"Oh, my God!"* sort of situation can happen any time.

In this scenario, you find yourself doing a not-so-hot job of "controlled braking." In fact, you've really messed it up, locking up the front wheels, while turning the steering wheel and making the front-end swerve.

Think of all this as a religious experience. At this point, your only salvation is to get that foot *off* the brakes. Once you have locked up your front wheels and subsequently decided that moving the car you are in out of the path of the oncoming obstacle is suddenly your major goal in life, you must take your foot *off* the brakes in order to get back the *steering control* you need to make that goal a reality.

ABS BRAKING

Here's the bad news: A study conducted in the US indicates that cars with anti-lock brakes are up to 65% more likely to be in fatal crashes than cars without them.

> But it's not the ABS that's the problem. It's poor driving habits and *lack of driver awareness on how the brakes operate.*

Let's take a step-by-step look at the braking process for an ABS vehicle *during emergency braking*:

- In an emergency situation, **apply your brakes hard and stay on them.** (Unlike in a non-ABS vehicle, pressing harder won't cause problems.)

- You **should not pump the brake pedal at any time on an ABS system.** Pumping could interrupt operation and actually increase stopping distance.

- **Hard application of ABS brakes will cause the brake pedal to vibrate or pulsate.** That's a good thing; don't let the vibration bother you. The pedal is *supposed* to vibrate. It lets you know the system is working.

- Along with the vibration, **you will hear a strange groaning noise** — don't let that bother you, either — it's *supposed* to make that noise.

- A **periodic decrease in brake pedal pressure** may occur.

> The best thing you can do is read the "Owner's Manual" and get familiar with what will happen when you really need the ABS.

BRAKE FAILURE

Probably the most frightening thing that can happen to you as a driver is to lose braking control *completely.* Your brakes just fail to do *anything* — they don't help you stop and they don't lock up.

Imagine it: You push down on the pedal and nothing, absolutely nothing, happens. **ABS or non-ABS — if you have no brakes, it does not matter *what* type of braking system you have.** The car just keeps on going.

This situation calls for quick decision making, especially if you are in a busy traffic environment, such as a crowded street, surrounded by plenty of large objects to collide with.

- Your best option is to **steer to avoid obstacles**, use **low gear** to slow the vehicle, and **seek a path of escape.**

- **Using the parking brake is an option,** but the parking brake only stops the *rear* wheels. If you *do* opt to use the parking brake, apply it slowly, keeping the front wheels pointed straight ahead. Any movement of the wheel while applying the parking brake will spin the car around 180 degrees.

BRAKE FADE

Brake fade occurs when brakes are overused and overheat. Hot brakes quickly lose their effectiveness and fail to stop the car in time. Brake fade comes and goes. Brakes take time to overheat and will often provide warning that they are about to fade. Effectiveness decreases slowly.

No matter the circumstances, brake fade makes it advisable to slow down. Brake fade goes away as the brakes cool. This often confuses drivers who experience brake fade. Sometimes they lose their brakes due to fade and run their cars off the road and into the under brush. Shaken but unscathed, they later return to their cars with a repair crew, only to find their brakes in mysteriously good working order. This is typical of brake fade.

PRACTICE MAKES PERFECT

If all this braking technique sounds like something to practice, it is. The questions are: where and when?

> The time to experiment with your car's braking characteristics is *not* while approaching a tractor-trailer truck stalled in your lane while you're traveling at 75 mph.

- **If you happen to live in an area that gets ice and snow in the winter,** find a big, empty parking lot, such as those at shopping malls or large supermarkets, and practice.

- **In a non-ABS vehicle,** see how hard you can press on the brake pedal *without* locking up the wheels.

- **In an ABS vehicle,** get the feel for the sensations of braking with an ABS. (See p. 183)

- **Watch out for light stanchions and parked cars** (we said find an *empty* lot), but **otherwise take it easy and carefully play with your car.** Discover its — and your own — limitations and abilities.

ELECTRONIC STABILITY CONTROL

It was only a matter of time before the cars we drive had computers that help us stay out of trouble. Computer aided driving is not new. ABS and Traction Control have been around for a while and add a great deal to the safety of a vehicle. Now there is a new device that adds to vehicle safety, it is called **Electronic Stability Control (ESC)**.

This device is as advertised when it comes to preventing accidents. Researchers at the Insurance Institute for Highway Safety found that Electronic Stability Control (ESC) reduces the risk of fatal multiple-vehicle crashes by 32 percent. The new research confirms that ESC reduces the risk of all single-vehicle crashes by more than 40 percent fatal ones by 56 percent. Researchers estimate that if all vehicles had ESC, as many as 10,000 fatal crashes could be avoided each year.

Electronic Stability Control uses the ABS and Traction Control computers to monitor what the car is doing, after you tell it what to do. By measuring throttle position, steering wheel angle and lateral acceleration, the computer compares the intended path of the vehicle to the path the car is actually taking. If it's not doing what you wanted it to do, or if what you are doing is contrary to good sense and the laws of physics, the ESC computer takes over. When ESC decides to handle the driving chores it applies one of the front brakes, or in some systems one of the front and/or rear brakes, to straighten the car and put it back on the path you want it on.

For those of us who have lost control of a car, we know that it's that first twitch of the car that tells us that we are about to have an exciting experience. That twitch is information the car is sending to us. For some, interpreting this information is second nature, and for others it's like trying to understand Swahili. That sinking feeling we get in our stomach is the car telling us that it's not going where we want it to go, but it is going in a path that it wants to go. The value of ESC is that it interprets the information, in most cases, before the average driver or even the above average driver can sense the problem. Once the ESC computer reads the information it starts to set the car on the correct path before we can figure out what's going on.

Helpful websites: The Insurance IInstitute for Highway Safety site features a video demonstrating ESC:

www.iihs.org/news/2006/iihs_news_061306.pdf

Find out which cars have ESC at:

www.aiadalists.org/newsroom/newsDetails.aspx?id=57205

Chapter 20

Turning:

How to Turn Left, Turn Right, Back Up and Turn Around

In Ch. 16 we covered the techniques for turning curves and corners *at speed* — on the open highway, at exit and entrance ramps, or in emergency driving situations. In this chapter, we focus on the simpler rules for turning in general — turning left, turning right, turning around, and backing up.

> **A proper signal of *intention* to turn right or left will be given *continuously* during not less than the last 100 feet traveled by the vehicle *before* turning.**

TURNING LEFT

Sometimes when you are making a left turn at an intersection, a passenger sitting beside you on the front seat will obstruct your vision of traffic coming from the right. If your vehicle is equipped with individual bucket seats, adjusting the passenger seat several inches backward of the driver's seat will give you a better view to the right. If the vehicle has a standard seat, you may have to lean forward to see around your passenger. If necessary, ask him to lean back to give you a better view.

When turning left:

- Be sure there is enough space to turn left.

- Signal your intent to turn and slow down.

- If there are two left turn lanes, take the right-hand turn lane.

- Be sure you are in the center of the intersection. Start to turn only *after* you are sure your vehicle's rear will clear the centerline.

- Be sure there is an adequate gap to turn in front of traffic.

- Watch your vehicle's progress in the side mirrors.

- Steer the vehicle wide of the lane, if necessary.

- When the vehicle's wheels are into the lane, steer left to put the vehicle in the lane and straighten up.

- If applicable, watch for oncoming traffic.

TURNING RIGHT

When making a right turn:

- Be sure there is enough space to turn right.

- Signal your intent to turn at least 100 feet ahead of the intersection, and slow down *gradually* as you approach the turn.

- Be sure to let oncoming traffic clear before you make your turn.

- Stay as close as possible to the right edge of the road or street.

- Never swerve to the left before turning right.

- Position your vehicle in the right-hand lane. Keep your vehicle's rear close to the curb.

- Do not turn wide to the left as you start the turn; the driver behind you might think you are turning left.

- Pull forward into the intersection past the right corner. You must do this so the vehicle's rear wheels can clear the curb. Turn the steering wheel hard to the right.

- Check your vehicle's progress using the right side mirrors.

- Watch oncoming cars if swinging wide into the left or oncoming lane.

- If the speed is right, the turn should be easily made without swerving.

- **If your tires squeal when you turn,** it is likely that you are trying to take the turn too fast, or tire pressures are too low.

BACKING UP

Far too many accidents happen while the car is in reverse. More often than not, these result in fender benders, not dramatic accidents, but nonetheless annoying and expensive. (We're going to cover backing up before turning around, because all the techniques for turning around — except the U-turn — involve backing up at some point.)

Cars Are Designed to Go *Forward*

Automobile suspensions possess a quality known as "caster" — the force that helps to straighten out the front wheels after turning a corner. Caster also gives the car stability while traveling forward.

Unfortunately, this stabilizing forward force *de-stabilizes* the car while it's in reverse. In other words, while driving in reverse, the steering wheel will not center automatically if you loosen your grip on it, as it will when in forward motion. Another little quirk of caster is that **the car becomes *unstable* while traveling backwards** — when small changes in steering wheel movement cause *big* changes in the way the car reacts to your inputs. Of course, the faster you go in reverse, the more difficult control becomes.

Key Points to Keep in Mind When Backing Up

- **No matter how short the distance you wish to travel in reverse, look where you're going and drive slowly.** Most cars feature a blind spot or spots to the rear large enough to hide a small child. Blow your horn. But whatever you do, **be absolutely sure there is no one behind you when you back up.**

- **Before you put the car in reverse, make sure the area in *front* of the car is clear.** Some cars have long hoods and broad front ends. As you maneuver backwards and turn, the noses of **many large cars swing out to the side dramatically** and you could hit something — or someone. Many cars in American today have badly dented fenders because drivers neglected to perform this check.

- **Try not to back into an intersection that contains a lot of traffic**.

- **Make sure you are able to reach all your car's controls.** It's a little foolish to hike yourself up in the seat for good visibility, put the car into reverse, and then discover you can't reach the brake pedal!

- **If you are backing up to the right, look over your right shoulder.** For comfort, you may put your right arm up on the back of the seat.

- **Short people have a hard time backing up** because they have a hard time seeing over the back of the front seat and out the rear window. If you are short, position yourself as best as you can, making certain that you can see out the rear window and access all the car's controls.

- While this may sound a bit foolish, **make sure the car has come to a complete halt before you put it in reverse.** Dropping an expensive transmission out of a car by slamming it into reverse can ruin your whole day.

- **Keep a foot on the brake while putting the car in reverse.** There's nothing like shooting out of a parking space and into the path of an oncoming car to add a little spice to daily life.

- **Another problem with backing up is knowing what to do with the steering wheel.** The correct direction in which to move the wheel while in reverse can be very confusing.

  Actually, the problem is mainly perceptual. **The correct way to move the wheel is really quite simple:** Move the top of the steering wheel in the direction you wish the car to move. It's actually no different from what you do while driving forward; it just feels different in reverse.

- **Never combine a great deal of steering wheel movement with a heavy foot on the gas pedal.** You will surely lose control of the car.

- **Use smooth applications of the brake, steering wheel, and accelerator.**

TURNING AROUND

We're going to look at three ways of turning around or changing direction. No matter what method is used, it must be done carefully. Know the legalities in your area concerning direction changes. Perform these turns in a "safe area" — that is, one having good visibility.

Before attempting the turn, make sure you have a clear view of the road(s) and traffic around you. Obviously you should avoid making turns on hills, curves, and near blind intersections. The three ways to reverse direction are:

- U-turns

- Two-point turns

- Three-point turns

U-Turns

The U-turn is the safest of the three turns. Keep in mind that the U-turn *should* be legal, but *isn't* universally. Although the U-turn is an easy turn to execute, you still need a lot of road and good visibility.

- **The average passenger vehicle needs about 40 feet in which to turn**, so you're going to need at least that much room.

- You should *not* make a U-turn unless **a vehicle approaching from either direction can see the movement from a distance of 500 feet.**

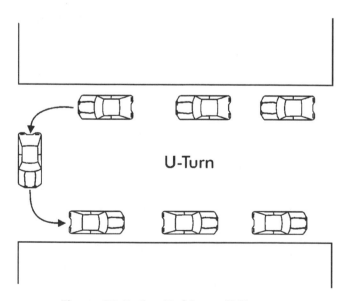

Figure 20-1. Car Making a U-Turn.

To make a proper U-turn:

- First **stop as close to the right side of the road as possible.** This gives you more room in which to execute the turn.

- **Look both ways** before you even begin to turn the steering wheel and start the turn.

- **Let everyone around you know what you're going to do.** Use your left-turn signal to indicate what you're planning.

- When you're *sure* everyone has been notified, **turn the wheel as quickly as possible and as sharply as necessary,** and complete the turn.

- Before pulling out and heading off in the other direction, make sure to **look over your shoulder and check for oncoming traffic.**

Two-Point Turns

A two-point turn means backing into a driveway, side road, or alley in order to make a 180-degree turn when the highway is too narrow, or there isn't enough visibility to make a U-turn, or a U-turn is illegal.

There are two basic ways of driving through a two-point turn: The right-hand road turn and its left-hand brother. The left-hand turn is much more dangerous than the right-hand turn.

The right road turn

The right road turn requires you to stop the car, back it into a road or driveway on the right side of the highway on which you are traveling, and then drive out onto the highway and make your turn.

- **Signal your intention to stop the car.**

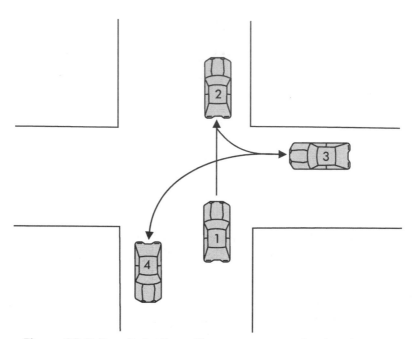

Figure 20-2. Two-Point Turn. These turns are made when the road is too narrow, or restricted visibility does not permit a U-turn, or a U-turn is illegal.

- Before you move backwards, **check to make sure that the path behind you is clear.**

- Be especially watchful for pedestrians.

- Then **back up slowly.** Remember: It is very easy to lose control of the car while traveling in reverse.

- **Before re-entering the traffic again,** make sure you can do so safely.

The left road turn

The left-hand variant of this turn requires the driver to drive nose-first into a road or driveway on the left side of the road, then back onto the highway, straighten out, and drive off.

- **Signal your intention to stop,** as well as **your intention to make a left-hand turn** onto the side road or driveway.

- **The most dangerous moment in this turn is when you are backing into oncoming traffic.** Watch out for this oncoming flow, and make sure all is clear in front of you before moving out into the traffic. Exercise due caution.

Three-Point Turn

The *three-point turn* should be made only where there is no other choice. Use this turn when the road is too narrow for a U-turn and there are no side roads or driveways that allow a two-point turn.

To perform a three-point turn:

- First **pull over and get as close to the right side of the road as possible**, just as if you were doing a U-turn.

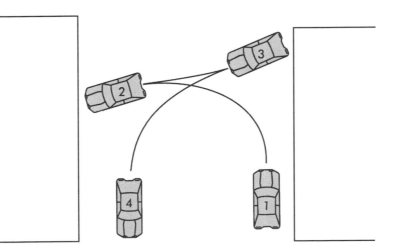

Figure 20-3. Three-Point Turn. Very dangerous turn-around; should not be used unless there is no other way of changing direction.

- **Turn your car as though you were going to do a U-turn** and follow all the standard U-turn precautions described above.

- **Just before the front wheels of your car reach the far side of the road,** turn the steering wheel to the right, check ahead and behind for oncoming traffic, put the car in reverse, and back up across both lanes.

> *Remember:* **Whenever the car is moving backwards, you should be looking the same way.**

- **Just prior to reaching the other side of the road, turn the wheel to the left.**

- **Drive forward.**

You have performed a three-point turn. It's a dangerous way of reversing direction because you are vulnerable to conflicting traffic for far too long a time. Unfortunately, sometimes there's no other way.

IN THE NEXT CHAPTER, we discuss the techniques for passing and being passed safely — when to pass, when NOT to pass, how to pass, and how to yield the right of way.

Chapter 21

Passing and Being Passed

You must decide whether to pass or not to pass again and again every time you drive. Do not take chances. Do not move out into the left-hand lane as soon as you see any possibility of getting by the vehicle ahead. On the other hand, do not let opportunities for safe passing go by while irritably following a slow-moving vehicle for mile after mile.

Safe passing depends mainly on your knowing three things:

- When to pass

- When *not* to pass

- How to pass safely

WHEN *NOT* TO PASS

When it comes to passing, there are some *NEVERS* — situations where passing is *always* dangerous or *unlawful:*

- *Never* pass when you cannot see that the left side of the road is free of oncoming traffic far enough ahead to pass safely.

- *Never* pass on any curve or hill where you cannot see at least 500 feet.

- Never pass at night when you can't see far ahead.

- *Never* pass unless you have sufficient distance to pass and return to the right without coming within 100 feet of an approaching vehicle.

- *Never* pass at an intersection.

- *Never* pass at a railway crossing.

- *Never* pass when there is a single or double solid line between lanes or when your lane's side of a double line is solid.

- *Never* pass at crosswalks where a vehicle has stopped to allow a pedestrian to cross.

- *Never* pass when a stopped school bus has its warning flashers on.

WHEN TO PASS

The question of whether or not to pass is never an easy one. Before you decide to pass someone, always think *before* you make your move — because if you recklessly pass someone, you (and perhaps others) will suffer the consequences. And always be especially wary of passing in traffic.

Here are some questions to ask yourself before making a move to pass:

1. **Is this pass really necessary?** Why do I want to pass this car? Is the maneuver absolutely necessary?

   If you want to pass someone who is slowing you down by driving slowly themselves, then passing is justified.

   If you need to pass the car ahead of you because there is an actual emergency, and you have to get where you're going in a hurry, then passing is justified.

   But if you want to pass because your ego just can't stand to have anyone ahead of you, then passing is NOT justified.

2. **Is this pass legal?** Although no responsible driver would or should pass illegally on purpose, there may be

an emergency situation where you *must* pass someone — especially if you're an emergency worker or working in an emergency capacity. If you *must* pass illegally in such circumstance, make especially sure you have enough time and space to make it. **If you are involved in an accident while making an illegal pass, you're in *BIG* trouble.**

3. **Is the car you are about to pass aware of your presence?** *Don't* assume this car is aware of your presence. *Don't* assume that the driver is in any condition to react rationally.

4. **Are there side roads ahead that may hide a car about to turn into your path?** Even if you can't see them, *assume* they're there. Use Murphy's Law and proceed, but with caution.

5. **Does the road have many intersections that can often conceal surprises,** such as other cars making turns or proceeding through the intersection? Watch out.

6. **Have you checked the traffic situation all around you in your mirrors?** Someone may be trying to pass *you.* Moreover, it's just good sense to check your mirrors before you make *any* move with your car.

7. **If there is an oncoming car, how far away is it?** Do you *really* have enough time and space?

8. **Are you sure your vehicle has the mechanical ability to make this pass safely?** Some cars aren't as powerful as they should be. Sometimes the luck of the draw gives you one that might be in need of a tune-up or have some other small mechanical problem that could inhibit performance. *Know you have the accelerating power before you need it.*

9. **How long is all this going to take**? Do you have enough time to pass and get back in your lane?

Of course, it's impossible to get out a yardstick and measure the distances involved. Estimating whether or not the pass is safe requires quick thinking. You haven't got much time. Your best friend here is your own good sense and your experience as a good driver. But if you have to make a mistake, make it on the side of too much caution, instead of not enough.

(See the section on *Safe Passing Distances*, p. 201.)

10. **Can your vehicle stop quickly and safely if you have to make an emergency stop?** (See Ch. 17, *Speed and Safe Stopping Distances*.)

Head-on collisions represent a substantial number of accidents.

If you *MUST* pass someone, realize and remember that, depending on the highway situation, you and your car are going to be spending a good deal of time in the *wrong lane*.

If you are traveling at 50 mph, passing someone going 40 mph, you will need about 10 seconds and 736 feet to safely complete the pass. If the crest of a hill is just 300 feet away, and there's a car just out of sight on the other side of that hill, you're going to have some problems on your hands — soon!

HOW TO PASS SAFELY

Signaling Your Intent to Pass

First of all, when passing, do not just pull out and start around the car you're trying to pass. Look ahead and behind to be sure it is safe to pass.

Signaling the driver AHEAD of you

Let the driver of the vehicle ahead know what you intend to do. She may be getting ready to pass the vehicle ahead of her or to turn left.

- **Blow your horn as a signal to her.** The horn signal is required by *law* in most localities, and it puts the driver of the vehicle being passed under *a legal obligation to help you pass.*

- **At night, give the driver ahead an *additional* signal by flashing your headlights from low to high beam and back to low.** However, do not use the light signal as a substitute for the horn signal.

Signaling the driver BEHIND you

The driver of the vehicle *behind* you also needs to know what you are going to do. He may be pulling out to pass *you.*

- Give a **left-turn signal** to let him know that you are about to pull out to pass.

Safe Passing Distance

You cannot pass safely unless you can see far enough ahead to be sure that you can get back in line before you meet any traffic coming from the opposite direction. You must also be able to get back into line before meeting any traffic crossing or turning onto the road on which you are driving.

But how far ahead is far enough? Give yourself and the driver of the vehicle you are passing *plenty of room*. This distance depends on you own speed, on the speed of the vehicle you are passing, and on the lengths of the vehicles involved.

- **Start to pass from a safe following distance.** If the vehicle you want to pass is traveling at 30 mph, start from at least 60 feet behind it.

> **Do *not* speed up directly behind a vehicle and then turn out suddenly just before you get to it.**

Remember: A driver who tailgates does not give himself enough time or distance to handle emergency situations.

Tailgating interferes with your view of the road ahead. The other driver may slow down or stop, and he can do so much more quickly than you can because his speed is lower. If he does, you will almost certainly be unable to slow down or stop in time. If you try to avoid a collision by turning sharply aside, you may skid off the road, turn over, or smash into another vehicle.

- **Drift over to the left and speed up quickly.**

- As you go by another vehicle, **be sure there is plenty of distance between the right side of your vehicle and the left side of the other vehicle.**

> **The law in most localities requires a *minimum clearance of two feet.***

- You have not finished passing until you **get back onto your own side of the road or in the lane where you belong,** leaving the vehicle you have just passed at **a safe following distance *behind* you.**

For example, if the vehicle you are passing is traveling at 30 mph, leave 60 feet clear before returning to your own side of the road (20 feet for every 10 mph of speed).

> **If you force the driver of the vehicle you have just passed to slow down as you get back into line, you have *not* passed safely.**

- Of course, **it is difficult to see the vehicle you have just passed and estimate the distance.**

> **A good rule of thumb is that you can usually be sure it is safe to return to the right side of the road when you can see the vehicle you have passed in your rearview mirror.**

- As a general rule, **do not attempt to pass more than one vehicle at a time.**

   Passing several vehicles increases the danger because it increases the time you spend and the distance you cover while out of your *own* lane.

- **If you come up behind a long line of vehicles,** you can almost be sure that *every* driver except the first one is waiting for an opportunity to pass. The safe and courteous thing to do is to *wait your turn.*

- On the other hand, **if you are next in line behind a slow-moving vehicle,** it is *discourteous* to the drivers behind you *not* to pass when you have the opportunity.

Safe Passing Speeds

And just how fast should you pass someone? Neither too fast, nor too slow. But how fast is too fast? And how slow is too slow?

For example: Suppose that you want to pass a vehicle that is traveling at 30 mph. You would have to travel whatever distance *it* travels while you are passing, plus an *additional* distance besides. Since the other vehicle's speed is 30 mph, the *additional* distance in this case would be about 160 feet.

- It is generally a good idea to **pass at a speed at least 10 to 15 mph faster than the speed of the vehicle being passed.**

- **If your speed is only 5 mph faster,** it will take you twice the time and almost twice the distance to completely pass the other vehicle.

- On the other hand, **there is no point in passing at too fast a speed.** In passing at 20 mph faster instead of 15 mph faster than the speed of the vehicle being passed, the advantage amounts to only 1 or 2 seconds gained. It is usually offset by the danger of increased speed.

- **If too much increased speed is *required* to pass and return to your lane,** the wise decision is not to pass.

- Similarly, **when the driver ahead of you is traveling just *under* the speed limit,** the safest thing to do is forget about passing.

  For example: Suppose that you want to pass a vehicle traveling at 50 mph when the speed limit is 55 mph. In this case, driving your vehicle 10 to 15 mph faster would be unlawful because passing is no excuse for exceeding the speed limit. Yet if you pass at 55 mph, you will need 2,640 feet or exactly half a mile to pass the other vehicle.

  So, the best thing to do is settle down behind him at a safe following distance. You may reach your destination a few minutes later than if you had attempted to pass, but at least you will not have broken the law.

SPECIAL PASSING SITUATIONS

Passing on Three-Lane Highways

Passing on a three-lane highway demands extra caution.

- **Do not pass except in the center lane, and then only when the center lane is marked for passing in *your* direction.** In some cases, the center lane may be so marked that it is open for passing in *both* directions.

- Before passing, **make sure that none of the vehicles coming from the *opposite* direction are moving out to pass.**

- **Never use the center lane to pass if your view of the road ahead is obstructed** by a hill or curve.

- The one exception to using only the center lane for passing is that **you may pass in the right lane if the vehicle in the center lane is making a left turn.**

Passing on the Right

Passing on the right, except as noted above, is usually dangerous and unlawful. It puts you on the other driver's blind side. He may be intending to make a right turn or to pull over to the right side of the road. In either case, an accident is almost certain.

There are, however, three situations in which passing on the right is usually permissible and reasonably safe:

1. If the highway has at least two lanes going in each direction.

2. If all lanes of traffic move in the same direction (one-way street).

3. If the vehicle you are passing is in a left-turn lane.

BEING PASSED

When you are being passed, *the law requires you to help the other driver get by.*

Give Way to the Right

- When the driver of the passing vehicle blows his horn, you must do one thing — **give way to the right.**

  Even if you are already on your own side of the road, move over as close as safety will permit to the right-hand edge of the road.

Maintain a Steady Speed

- **When you are being passed, it is usually safest to maintain a steady speed.** By doing this, you allow the passing driver to judge passing distance with greater accuracy. If you *slow down*, you may mislead the passing driver into overestimating his speed.

- **The law does not permit you to *increase* your speed when you're being passed.** Speeding up forces the passing driver to cover more distance and take more time to get by you. **It exposes both of you to unnecessary danger.**

- **If an attempt to pass you becomes dangerous,** you may be able to **make it safer for everyone by *slowing* down** and allowing the passing vehicle to get back into the proper lane in less time and distance.

- If, however, you see that **a driver is trying to get back into line behind you, rather than ahead of you, do *not* slow down.** In this case, it is much safer to speed up a little to give him more room.

How to Merge Onto the Highway Without Crashing

The following is a description of how you should merge onto a highway safely and without endangering or harming yourself or others.

Steps

- **Make sure you are going at the same speed as the traffic you are merging with** before you hit the point at which the ramp merges with the highway. This is very important so that those coming up behind you on the highway do not hit you from behind.

- **Put your turn signal on** so that the cars on the highway knows you are merging into their lane.

- **Look first in your driver's side rearview mirror and then quickly glance out towards the left** (when driving in right-side driving countries) and behind you to see if there is any car in your blind spot (the blind spot is the spot that every car has where you cannot see who is really close to you but one lane over behind you).

- **Determine if you have room to merge onto the highway,** if you do not (a car is currently beside you) you will have to speed up or down until you have ample space to merge into.

- **Gradually, never abruptly, merge into the lane**, following the natural path of the merging ramp. Make sure to maintain your speed, which should be the same speed as the cars in the right lane on the highway.

Tips

- Look at the highway traffic flow as soon as possible in order to help you determine the opening you will want to accelerate into

- Always turn your head and look, don't just use the rearview mirror, as you will miss cars in your blind spot.

- Make sure you are going fast enough to merge safely.

- Pay attention and do not be distracted by other things

- If you are really nervous and there are others in the car, ask them to be quiet so you can focus.

- Try to merge into traffic with at least one car length of space in front and behind of your vehicle.

- Remember to check if you can stay in the lane you have just merged into. In many major cities, the right-most lane is a commuter lane that is only open during certain hours. Always keep an eye on how much of the merge lane remains. Merge lanes, even on the same highway can vary greatly in length.

- If you cannot merge onto the highway, and have the option to exit, do so. You can always loop around and try again.

Warnings

- Don't forget to put your turn signal on. It is the best signal to the traffic in the merging lane of what you are about to do.

- Sometimes, there may be no merge area at the end of the ramp. This will be clearly indicated by signs such as "No Merge Area" or "Yield". In this case you might have to slow down or even stop to make sure you are going to merge into an empty spot in the next lane.

- Remember that other drivers may be behind you and are also trying to merge. Try to provide them space to merge into as well, by moving another lane over if possible.

- Watch out for vehicles merging into your lane. Many entrances onto a highway are also the exit for the road you just came from.

When danger develops in passing, do not stand on your rights. Use all driving skills to avoid an accident.

PART III

ACCIDENTS

In the first two Parts, we've covered in detail what you need to know and be able to do to keep yourself and your vehicle under control while on the road. We've also shown you how, in some cases, to regain control if you lose it. But accidents *do* happen — either we, or the drivers around us on the road, don't maintain control — or we, or they, can't regain it.

So in this Part, we look at current accident statistics to see the who, what, when, and how of accidents. Then we explore what causes accidents (driver, environment, vehicle). Then we consider typical accident scenarios and tell you how to deal with them. And finally we offer a "Crash Course" that provides some suggestions on how you can help if you come upon or are involved in an accident yourself.

Chapter 22

Accident Stats:

Who, What, When, and How

In 1975, the US Department of Transportation started **an annual census of motor vehicle deaths,** recording information on crash type, vehicle type, road type, driver characteristics, and a variety of other factors. Institute researchers analyze these data each year to quantify the public health problem of motor vehicle deaths.

Based on analysis of **data from the U.S. Department of Transportation's Fatality Analysis Reporting System (FRS):**

- A total of 42,815 people lost their lives in motor vehicle crashes in 2002. Another 3.0 million people were injured.

- Motor vehicle crashes are the leading cause of death among Americans 1-34 years old.

- The total societal cost of crashes exceeds $150 billion annually.

- Contributing to the death toll are alcohol, speed, and various other driver behaviors, plus the kinds of vehicles people drive and the roads on which they travel.

- The majority of persons killed or injured in traffic crashes were drivers (65%) followed by passengers (30%), pedestrians (3%) and pedalcyclists (2%).

Gender

- **More men than women die each year in motor vehicle crashes.** Men typically drive more miles than women and engage more often in risky driving practices, including not using a safety belt, driving while impaired by alcohol, and speeding.

- However, **deaths of female drivers have increased during the past 20 years while male driver deaths have declined.** More women now are licensed than in the past. They drive more miles and are more likely to be driving at night.

- **One-third of all motor vehicle deaths in 1998 were females.** They accounted for 31 percent of driver deaths, 50 percent of passenger deaths, 32 percent of pedestrian deaths, 13 percent of bicyclist deaths, and 9 percent of motorcyclist deaths.

Age

- The motor vehicle death rate per 100,000 people is especially **high among 16-24 year-olds** and **people 80 years and older.**

- The difference is **least among people younger than 13** and **greatest among people 85 years and older.**

- The difference is **greatest among people age 85 and older,** followed closely by **people age 20-24.**

Age/Gender Differences

- **At all ages, males have much higher motor vehicle death rates** per 100,000 people compared with females.

- The **highest motor vehicle death rate is among males 80 years and older,** followed closely by **males age 16-24.**

- The death rate is **highest among males age 85 and older,** and it is **lowest among males and females younger than 16.**

- **At almost all ages, males have higher passenger vehicle death rates than females.**

- There is **no gender difference among people younger than 16.**

Alcohol Involvement

- Among passenger vehicle drivers in 2002, the proportion of fatally injured males with **blood alcohol concentrations (BACs) at or above 0.10** percent was higher than females at all ages.

- **Alcohol was most common among males age 21-30** and **females 31-40,** when half of male deaths and about one-third of female deaths involved high BACs.

- Since 1980, **proportions of fatally injured drivers with BACs at or above 0.10 percent** have **declined 36 percent among men and 56 percent among women.**

- Since 1985, **the percentage of male driver deaths with high BACs has been about twice that of females.**

Vehicle Types

- **Fifty percent of motor vehicle deaths** in 2002 were **car occupants.**

- **Fourteen percent were occupants of other kinds of passenger vehicles** including pickups, utility vehicles, and cargo/large vans.

Box 22-1. **Passenger Vehicle Fatalities**

By far the largest number of motor vehicle deaths are occupants of passenger vehicles, including cars, the popular passenger vans (often referred to as minivans), pickups, utility vehicles, and cargo/large passenger vans.

> **NOTE: If the wheelbase of a car fits one size group, but the overall length fits another size group, the vehicle is grouped in the larger category. Passenger versions of vans often referred to as minivans are classified as cars.**

The likelihood of crash death varies markedly among these vehicle types according to size.

- **Small/light vehicles** have less structure and size to absorb crash energy, so more injurious forces can reach their occupants in crashes.

- People in **lighter vehicles** are at a disadvantage in collisions with heavier vehicles.

- **Pickups and utility vehicles** are proportionally more likely than cars to be in fatal single-vehicle crashes, especially rollovers.

- However, **pickups and utility vehicles** generally are heavier than cars, so occupant deaths are less likely to occur in multiple-vehicle crashes.

- **Deaths in pickups and utility vehicles have more than doubled** since 1975.

- Since 2001, **deaths per registered vehicle have declined in all kinds of passenger vehicles.**

- **Forty six percent of passenger vehicle occupant deaths** in 2002 were **car occupants.**

- However, **the proportion of deaths involving pickup and utility vehicle occupants is growing** as the popularity of these vehicles increases.

- Sixty percent of **car occupant deaths** in 2002 occurred in **single-vehicle crashes,** 40 percent in **multiple-vehicle crashes.**

- In contrast, percentages for **pickups and utility vehicles** combined were 59 and 41 percent.

Crash Types

- **Frontal impacts** accounted for 50 percent of passenger vehicle occupant deaths in 2002.

- **Side impacts** accounted for 30 percent (14 percent right side, 16 percent left).

- **Crashes in which a vehicle rolled over** accounted for 31 percent of passenger vehicle occupant deaths in 2002 (54 percent of single-vehicle crash deaths and 11 percent of multiple-vehicle crash deaths).

- **Frontal impacts** accounted for 65 occupant deaths per million registered passenger vehicles in 2002 compared with 45 deaths per million in side impacts and 7 deaths per million in rear impacts.

- **Multiple-vehicle crashes** accounted for 73 occupant deaths per million registered passenger

vehicles in 2002 compared with 70 deaths per million
in single-vehicle crashes.

- **In single-vehicle crashes,** two-wheel-drive utility
  vehicles had the highest number of deaths per
  registered vehicle (127 per million) in 2002.

- **In multiple-vehicle crashes,** cars had a higher
  number of deaths per registered vehicle (80 per
  million) than pickups and utility vehicles.

- **Single-vehicle crashes involving rollover**
  accounted for 41 occupant deaths per million
  registered passenger vehicles in 2002 compared with
  11 deaths per million in **multiple-vehicle crashes.**

- **Single-vehicle rollover crashes** accounted for 50
  percent of occupant deaths in utility vehicles in 2002
  compared with 31 percent of deaths in pickups and 19
  percent of deaths in cars.

- **Lighter utility vehicles are disproportionately
  involved in fatal rollover crashes.** The
  single-vehicle rollover death rate in these vehicles in
  2002 was more than 5 times as high as the rate in the
  largest cars (110 deaths per million registered vehicles
  compared with 22).

IN THE NEXT CHAPTER, we explore the "Driving System" — the
driver, machine, and environment combination — and
consider how accidents can be caused by a breakdown in any
one part of the "system."

Chapter 23

What Causes Accidents?

The Driving System

Your ability to avoid accidents does not depend solely on your ability to control the car. When driving a car, you're at the mercy of the environment around you and at the mercy of the vehicle you are driving. Like Mother Nature, driving is a balance, and that balance is called the "driving system." The driving system is made up of three components: THE DRIVER, THE MACHINE, and THE ENVIRONMENT.

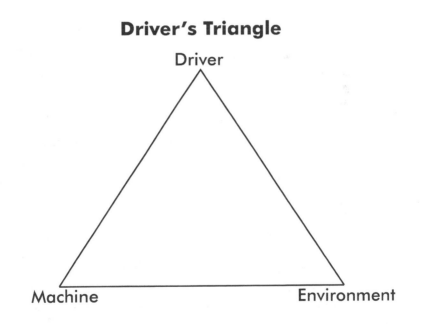

Driver's Triangle

Driver

Machine   Environment

Figure 23-1. The Driving System

When an automotive accident occurs, it is caused by a failure of the driving system. Either the driver, the vehicle, or the environment failed.

The Driver

The driver is the only truly flexible, adaptable factor of the driving system triangle. The driver is responsible for the successful implementation of the DRIVER/MACHINE relationship. If the driving system fails, only the driver suffers.

The proof lies in the numbers. **Some 89 percent of all vehicular accidents are caused by driver error** (this number is clouded by the fact that 48 percent of that 89 percent figure is directly attributable to accidents caused by drinking). But the remaining 41 percent were clear-headed drivers who somehow got into trouble.

The Machine

A little-known fact about cars is that **most of them are good handling vehicles.** However, no matter how well a vehicle handles, it is only a machine, and like all machines, **has its limitations.**

These limitations are aggravated when maintenance is poor or insufficient, but accidents caused by outright mechanical failure are relatively rare.

Accidents due to impaired vehicle performance due to poor or relaxed maintenance standards are difficult, if not impossible, to compute.

The Environment

The United States has the best-designed and constructed highway system in the world. Nevertheless, these **roads are not immune to the effects of weather and use.** If the road surface has been modified by nature, then the driver and machine portion of the driving system must cope with these changes.

In some rare instances the road conditions have deteriorated to the point that the driver/machine combination cannot compensate.

It is the environmental portion of the driving system that puts drivers at a distinct disadvantage. People drive in all sorts of weather conditions, when they do they are at the mercy of the environment. (See Ch. 26, *Foul Weather Driving.*)

The Driving Problem

Auto accidents are the fourth leading cause of death in the U.S. This figure gives us an idea of the size of the problem we are dealing with here. The biggest problem with driving is that we don't know *what* the problem is. From the numbers alone, it's obvious we're doing something wrong.

Yet, most people find it difficult to acknowledge their driving deficiencies. In fact, you'd be hard-pressed to find anyone who is willing to admit they have anything to learn about driving at all. Most of us went to some sort of high school driver education program, and then were tested by the local authorities. **After passing our written and road tests and receiving our license to drive, all of us assumed we had become instant *experts*.**

We were wrong. The simple fact is that **we all learn to drive through experience.** We become good or bad drivers through the types of driving experiences we have had. If we manage to survive these experiences, there is usually no problem.

The old "there's an infamous intersection near here where all the accidents happen" experience

It's an experience all drivers go through. We all have one intersection nearby that's known far and wide as a dangerous place to drive — the sort of intersection you're just plain lucky to survive. You probably have to drive through that intersection on your way to work, and when you do cross it, you do so with caution. Why? Because *experience* and local legend have taught you that this intersection is dangerous and deserves caution.

Types of Accidents

Accidents are not always accidental. They are an unexpected events that happens by chance — and are caused by **breakdowns in the driving system.** Through research it is possible to determine the cause of an accident. **Drivers must accept that most are caused by driver error.** Most drivers, unfortunately, are extremely unwilling to do this. People disassociate themselves from accidents. Drivers involved in accidents talk about them as though they weren't anywhere near the car when it crashed.

Consider the person who says, "*My car was hit by another car that went through a stop sign.*" To listen to this person, you'd think that no one was in either car at the time of the accident! **Cars don't drive past stop signs all by themselves.** Once we accept the fact that we can actually get *ourselves* into an accident, and that in most cases it will either be you or the other driver who is the cause of the accident, then the next important concept to understand is the type of accident we are likely to become involved *in*.

> **JUST HOW DO ACCIDENTS HAPPEN? If we know the types of driving conditions that produce the greatest number of accidents, then we can be more alert during these conditions.**

Two-car collisions

Ninety-six percent of all two-car collisions (excepting two-car fatal collisions) can be described as taking place under three separate conditions:

1. **The most frequent type of two-car collision is the side collision.** Out of all two-car collisions, 44.6 percent are side collisions. The most common type of two-car crash occurs when both cars are traveling in

parallel courses and one crosses the path and hits the side of the other.

2. **The second most frequent type of accident is the rear-end collision.** Some 27.7 percent of the accidents discussed here fall into this category. This usually happens when one vehicle is stopped and the second car, overtaking from the rear in a straight line, hits the stopped car. The second most common rear-end crash involves the striking vehicle hitting a *parked* car.

Box 23-1. The Top 10 Two-Car Crash Situations

1. Two cars traveling straight; one hits the side of the other (13.5 percent)

2. The striking vehicle traveling straight; it hits another vehicle making a left-hand turn (10.3 percent)

3. Vehicle proceeding in a straight line rear-ends a stopped vehicle (8.2 percent)

4. Vehicle traveling in a straight line hits the side of a vehicle that's just started to move(4.3 percent)

5. Hitting a parked car (4.2 percent)

6. Car out of control hits the rear of a stopped car (3.7 percent)

7. The striking vehicle, making a left turn, hits a vehicle head on (3.2 percent)

8. Two vehicles traveling straight and in opposite direction hit each other head on (3.1 percent)

9. Out of control vehicle hits the side of a vehicle making a lefthand turn (2.8 percent)

10. A car traveling in a straight line rear-ends a vehicle that is slowing down (2.6 percent)

3. **The third most common two-car accident type is a bit unusual.** Amounting to 13.6 percent of the two-car, non-fatal accidents, this is the kind of **head-on collision in which the two vehicles are not traveling straight toward each other.** In this category, the most common accident scenario involves a striking vehicle making a left-hand turn and impacting a car coming the other way head on.

The second most frequent type of head-on crash *does* involve both cars traveling in straight lines, directly at each other.

Single-car accidents

The statistics for single-car accidents are very different than those for two-car collisions. According to the figures, in some 50 percent of all single-car accident, the car was out of control *before* it hit anything or went off the road. This means that something happened to cause the driver to lose control.

Amazingly, **in 40 percent of the single-car mishaps, the car was traveling in a straight line before leaving the road.** For some reason, the drivers simply did not understand the problem or sense of the crisis in time to do anything about it, and just drove off the road. **In these straight-crash conditions, the drivers had various options of action, but instead did nothing.** Meaning, more than likely, that the driver didn't have a clue as to either what was happening, or how to get out of danger.

Obviously **some conditions are more conducive to single-car crashes.** Most happen:

- On slippery roads
- On curves
- On 55 mph roads

> **Statistics reveal that slippery conditions cause 45.8 percent of all single-car accidents — meaning that 54.2 percent of all single-car accidents take place on dry roads. Interestingly, 78.7 percent of *all* accidents happen on dry roads.**

Just what causes a no-control situation? Many complex factors affect loss of control of a vehicle. Generally, however, the no-control situation is induced by the driver.

Quite simply, the vehicle does not act in the manner to which the driver is accustomed. Usually, this happens when the driver *over* controls the car. **Over control can take several forms,** among them:

- Turning the steering wheel too much

- Applying the brakes too hard

- Stepping on the gas pedal too hard causing the rear wheels to spin resulting in loss of control

- A combination of the above

In any of these actions, the driver has put a demand on the vehicle that it cannot accept. If the vehicle cannot accept the demands, the vehicle goes out of control. (See all of Part II, *The Science and Techniques of Everyday Driving.*)

Accident-Producing Situations Caused by Drivers Themselves

Here are some examples of accident-producing situations that drivers get themselves into *through their own fault:*

1. **Tailgating.** Driving to close to the vehicle in front of you. When you do this, you won't have time to react if the other driver brakes, or if there is some other type of emergency.

2. **Making a sudden lane change, or a sudden change in speed.** All lane changing should be done as slowly as possible and by giving everyone around you plenty of warning that you are about to make a move.

   Admit it. You're often annoyed by drivers who zip from lane to lane, maneuvering about the highway as if they're the only ones on the road. *So don't do the same thing yourself!* Train yourself to never make a move with your car without first looking to see if someone is in the space you want to be in. And signal in plenty of time before you make that move.

3. **Failure to recognize when you are in trouble.** This is one of the toughest problems you'll face. There's not much you can do to train for this situation, because by the time you know you're in it, you may not be able to get out of it. The best thing for you to do is understand the different situations that can get you into trouble and be able to recognize them before they're inescapable.

4. **Not paying attention to the driving task.** Many times this is not because the driver is lazy, but occurs due to drowsiness, stress, and just daydreaming behind the wheel.

5. **Driving while emotionally unstable.** Never let your emotions get hold of you while driving. Driving while emotionally upset, especially while unusually angry or sad can reduce your ability to recognize danger and avoid it.

Accident-Producing Situations Caused by Defective Vehicles

Vehicle defects

Very few accidents are caused by a defective vehicle. In modern cars, this sort of catastrophic mechanical failure is practically nonexistent. Unfortunately, while a car may be constructed quite adequately for regular civilian, day-to-day driving, it might not be adequate for emergency drivers.

Almost all vehicle defects give the driver some advance warning that a failure is imminent. **Most people ignore the warning signs and keep on driving until there is a dramatic failure of the component or systems.** Luckily for these people, when the component or system does finally fail, the worst thing that generally happens is that the car stops and they have to wait for a tow-truck.

Tire defects

Tires are better than ever. Today's tires are state-of-the-art. But like any mechanical device, a tire will fail if not well treated. Suffice it to say that it's foolish to drive on badly worn tires. (See Ch. 8, *Tires, Part II* for tips on good tire care.)

Brakes defects

Don't wait until you have to toss out an anchor to stop the car, or until you can hear a metal-to-metal scraping when you hit the brakes. At the first sign of something unusual, have the brakes checked.

Vision restrictions

It is truly amazing to see the number of people that drive around with their windshields and rear windows completely covered with dirt. In order to drive, you have to see where you're going. Take the time to clean all your windows, and make sure the windshield wipers are in good working order. (See Ch. 4, *Windshields and Mirrors*, for tips on keeping your windshield and windshield wipers at their best.)

IN THE NEXT CHAPTER, we explore the basic accident situations you're likely to encounter on the road — as well as some specific dangers that you should watch out for and be prepared to handle. And, since you'll likely encounter not only vehicles, but pedestrians and bicyclists as well, we give you tips on how to safely "share the road."

Chapter 24

Typical Accident Scenarios:
And How to Deal with Them[1]

It's impossible to cover *all* the dangerous situations you can find yourself in when you're driving a car. But **a level-headed, quick-reacting defensive driver can do many things to avoid collisions and respond safely:**

- Many times you can avoid a collision merely by **slowing down.**

- Even after it is too late to stop or slow down, you may often avoid a collision by **swerving to one side.**

- It is normally **safer to swerve to the right than to the left.**

- It is **better to run off the road to the right than to collide head on.**

- However, **a speeding vehicle cannot be turned sharply without the risk of turning over.** The faster a vehicle is going, the more distance it takes to turn safely from a straight path.

- And a lot of dangerous situations can be avoided by simply **being more alert.**

Yield the Right of Way

A lot of accidents can be avoided if all drivers followed the rules of yielding the right of way. Always observe the rules of

---

[1] Sections in this chapter marked with * are copyright Shell Oil Company material and are reproduced with permission. Material was written by Mike Carpenter and in cooperation with the National Safety Council.

right-of-way with judgment and courtesy. Safe drivers give the right-of-way rather than taking it — even if the right of way is legally theirs.

- In general, **when two vehicles enter an intersection at about the same time,** the vehicle on the left yields the right-of-way to the vehicle on the right.

- **Always yield right-of-way to the first vehicle arriving at an intersection.**

- **When entering a through highway from a secondary road,** give the right-of-way to traffic on the main thoroughfare.

- **Fire, police, and emergency vehicles** have the right-of-way over all other vehicles.

BASIC ACCIDENT SITUATIONS

One of the basic points about avoiding accidents is easy to understand and very fundamental to safe driving: **Leave yourself an out — an escape route to every move you make.**

To do this, you have to **be aware of what's going on around you all the time.** Your best tools for doing this are your mirrors, both rearview and sideview. (Too many of us only use our rearview mirrors when we want to pull out into traffic.) Use all your mirrors in order to see the big picture — accurate information about what's going on on your right, left, and rear. In an emergency situation, such as a collision right in front of you, you need all the information you can get about what's happening around you, and you need it fast. Mirrors are your best way of getting this information.

Oncoming Car

Oncoming cars may cross the centerline and into your intended line of travel. They can move into your line of travel while making a left turn or while passing another vehicle. Even on freeways, where most drivers consider themselves safe from oncoming hazards, cars can cross medians or even jump guardrails. The results are head-on crashes.

- If you see a car coming at you in what looks like will be a head-on situation, **your two options are to change speed and/or change direction.**

- The best alternative is to **slow down and turn to the right.** It is far better to go off the road than to hit another vehicle head on. While you're moving to the right, **blow your horn.**

- Of course, **you must be aware of what you're turning into.** If the right side of the road is occupied by kids getting off a school bus, you really don't have much choice — your only alternative is to hit the car.

- **If you *must* move to the left,** remember that there's the chance that the oncoming driver might correct at the last minute and turn back *into* the direction you've just gone.

- **If you *can't* avoid a collision, brake firmly and steadily.** Every mile per hour you slow down will reduce the impact.

Entering & Merging

In these situations, cars can squeeze in on your path of travel at a slight angle from either side. Such vehicles are usually accelerating from either a standing or moving position. They may be changing lanes, or starting out from a parked position along the roadside.

Entering and merging is a common freeway occurrence, where cars merge from ramps and acceleration lanes.

- The major problem with the merging car is when it comes equipped with a driver that acts without looking. In this, as in all driving problems, there is no simple solution to the driver who acts and *then* looks.

- The only solution to this in the entering and merging scenario is to make sure the other driver sees *you*.

Be especially wary of drivers who pull away from parking spaces without looking.

- The best way to avoid this on a multi-lane street is to try to **stay in the middle or left lane.**

- Otherwise, **keep an eye peeled for parked cars with their front wheels canted in toward the street, and that have their brake lights on.** They're probably getting ready to pull out and may be in such a hurry they don't bother to look before they move.

Ongoing or Cars Ahead

Ongoing cars (that is, cars traveling in the same direction and at roughly the same speed you are) cause problems in two basic ways.

- The driver of the car ahead of you may **suddenly stop or swerve out of the lane** to avoid hitting another vehicle or object in the roadway. Either move on the other car's part can produce a collision.

- **Give the car ahead of you enough room to maneuver.** Do not tailgate.

When you're stopped in line at an intersection

Two special situations arise when you are stopped at an intersection.

You are the first car stopped at an intersection (with or without a stop sign).

You're waiting to make a left turn. Keep your front wheels pointed straight until it's time to make that turn. Why? Simple. If your wheels are turned left, and you're hit from the rear, your car will be pushed to the left because of the direction the front wheels are pointed. This move would put you directly in the path of oncoming traffic, with the potential of more collisions even more dangerous than the first.

You're the *second* car in line stopped at an intersection that has a stop sign.

The car in front of you pulls out. You look left and right for opposing traffic. It looks OK and you start to pull out, only to

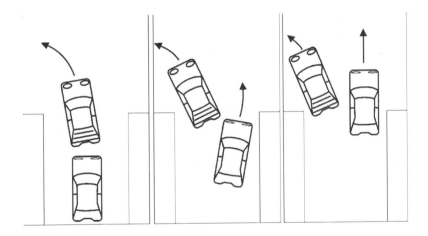

Figure 24-1. Avoiding a Car Stopped at an Intersection. The car ahead is stopped to make a left turn onto the main road. After pulling ahead somewhat, the car ahead slams on the brakes. Stop quickly if you can. If not steer to the car's right. Do not try to pass the other car; it may lead you into the path of oncoming cars that you cannot see.

Drawing and caption adapted from Medical Economics, by permission of the Medical Economics Company, Inc.

find that the driver in front of you has developed cold feet and stopped. You hit him from the rear.

- In this situation, patience is the key.

- Let the first car pull out and clear the intersection, then look both ways to see if it's safe for you to proceed. (See Figure 24-1, p. 233)

Car Following Too Closely

A car following you too closely, or closing in on you from behind at a high rate of speed, can crash into your vehicle's rear end should you need to stop suddenly. Tailgaters are always a serious problem, a problem made even worse at night. Fortunately, the solution to a tailgater is not too difficult — pull over and let the idiot go by.

Cars Backing Out

In an urban environment, people are prone to backing out of parking spaces without looking to see what's there. If they are heading toward you, a gentle toot on your horn will inform them that you are there and you'd greatly appreciate it if they would not back into you.

Motorcyclists*

Any time you see or hear a motorcyclist near you, be especially cautious. Motorcyclists are difficult to see because they're smaller than most vehicles. Statistics show that motorcyclists are about 16 times as likely as automobile occupants to die in a traffic crash.

Pedestrians and Bicyclists

Vehicles aren't your only problem. Pedestrians and bicyclists are potential challenges to your driving skills as well.

Intersecting pedestrian or bicyclist and vehicular traffic is a source of serious problems, despite the *many* control devices used to regulate their interaction. Intersections are the sites for a very high percentage of *all* collisions — including vehicles, pedestrians, and bicyclists. Moreover, pedestrians and bicyclists can come into your line of travel at almost *any* time. In general:

- **When you pull up to an intersection,** always look for conflicting traffic entering — vehicular, pedestrian, and bicyclist.

- **Even if you have the legal right of way,** it doesn't protect you from the physical reality of getting hit by a car whose driver just didn't see it your way, or your hitting a pedestrian who decided to cross the street without looking.

- In such situations you will probably not have **enough room or time to stop your car.** Therefore, you will need to know how to swerve out of harm's way and stop as quickly as possible.

Although many *bicyclists* **have experience riding in traffic and know how to watch out for cars and trucks, many** *motorists* **are NOT generally accustomed to bicyclists (and often pedestrians) on the road.**

Motorists should therefore learn how pedestrians and bicyclists are *required* **to use the road and how to** *share* **the road with them courteously and safely.**

The following tips for motorists on how to share the road with bicyclists and pedestrians are provided courtesy of Bike Florida and Florida's Share the Road Campaign, Lyndy Lyle Moore, www.bikeflorida.org.

Rules/regulations that bicyclists *and* pedestrians *must/should follow*

- **Bicyclists** *must* **obey the same traffic rules and regulations as motor vehicle drivers.** This means **they ride *with* traffic** (not facing it), and signal, make turns, and stop as any motor vehicle must.

- A bicyclist may ride on a sidewalk unless *forbidden* by local laws — this means than **in many areas bicyclists MUST use the same road as motorists.**

- **Between sunset and sunrise bicyclists** are *supposed* to have a white light on the front and a red reflector and a red light on the rear.

- Unlike bicyclists, **pedestrians should walk *facing* traffic at the edge of the road when there is no sidewalk present.**

- **Pedestrians *should* be visible at night** by wearing bright reflective clothing and carrying a flashlight.

- **Pedestrians *should* look in all directions** before stepping into the road, even at signalized crosswalks.

- **Pedestrians *should* be predictable and cross directly from curb to curb,** staying within the marked area or a straight pathway.

Because not all pedestrians and bicyclists (or drivers) follow the rules and regulations perfectly all the time, motorists must ALWAYS be prepared for the unexpected. People don't always do what you expect them to do!

Sharing the road with bicyclists and pedestrians

- Slow down in **school zones, parks, and residential areas** (areas very likely to have pedestrians and/or bicyclists in the roadway).

- Use extra caution during **peak morning and afternoon riding hours.**

- **When turning at an intersection,** with or without a signal, look for pedestrians and bicyclists crossing from all directions.

- **Yield to bicyclists and pedestrians at both marked and unmarked crosswalks** — especially when turning right on red.

- **Stop behind the stop bar at intersections,** not in the crosswalk, so pedestrians can cross the street safely.

- **Even though a bicyclist's pace may pose a momentary delay in your schedule,** it is important to respect the bicyclist's safety and *legal* right to the roadways.

- **Bicyclists' skills vary.** When possible, assess the rider's capabilities. A safe (experienced) rider holds a steady line.

- **Yield the right of way to a bicyclist** as you would a car.

- **Keep cool and lay off the horn and flashing headlights.** It's *sometimes* OK for a short "toot" to warn bicyclists, but do not BLAST your horn when approaching them — you could startle them and cause them to swerve or fall.

- **When passing a bicyclist,** reduce speed and allow three to five feet of passing space between your vehicle and the bicycle. Add one foot for every 10 mph over 50 mph.

- **A moving vehicle creates wind turbulence that can seriously affect a bicyclist's control.** When meeting or passing cyclists, slow down and give the widest berth possible. Crosswinds compound the problem for bicyclists.

- **Bicyclists worry about road defects you'd never feel in your car.** Allow them plenty of room in case they swerve to miss a pothole, storm drain, debris, or other obstacles.

- Bicyclists require extra courtesy while negotiating **railroad tracks and narrow bridges.**

- **On a two-lane road,** don't pass a bicyclist if oncoming traffic is near.

One Road, Many Users — Be Courteous and Share the Road.

OTHER DRIVING DANGERS*

Someone Runs a Red Light

Never assume a green light means all okay. There's little consolation in knowing an accident isn't your fault just because you had the right of way. Your car is still damaged, and someone may be hurt. Even though you were in the right, perhaps you could have actually avoided the collision simply by looking before you leaped.

- **If your light is green,** make sure other drivers, at or near the intersection, aren't trying to beat the yellow, or red.

- **If you're at an intersection *without* a light,** look left, right, and left again before moving out.

You Have a Blowout

If you slam on the brakes you could lose control completely.

- **If a front tire blows,** the car will pull hard to the side of the blowout. The steering wheel vibrates like crazy.

    1. **Hang on tight with your hands at the 9 o'clock and 3 o'clock positions** on the steering wheel.
    2. **Take your foot off the gas** and concentrate on staying in your lane.
    3. Then **slow down gradually and pull off the road** to a safe location.

- **If a rear tire blows,** the back of the car will weave back and forth and vibrate. But you should **handle it the same way as you would if a front tire blows.**

You Start to Skid

A lot of people hit the brakes hard when their car starts to skid. That generally makes things worse. (See Ch. 14, *Losing and Regaining Traction* for a thorough discussion of the different kinds of skids and how to handle them.) In general:

- Just **take your foot off the gas and turn your steering wheel in the direction you want the front of the car to go.** This helps straighten out the car and often regains traction.

- **Frequently it takes more than one turn of the steering wheel** to correct a skid.

Your Brakes Fail

You must think and act quickly. Remember this word-sequence: pump pedal, parking brake, shift down, safe place. (See Ch. 19, *Braking Control, Part II*, for a thorough discussion of braking techniques. See also p. 183)

1. **Pump the brake pedal.** Sometimes the pressure comes back. (Unless you have an ABS brake system. Never pump the brake pedal on ABS brakes.)

2. **Slowly try the parking brake.** But don't jam it on hard if you're in a curve. That could cause a spin.

3. **Shift into a lower gear** (or lower range on automatic transmissions). The drag on the engine will help slow you down. Do all three of these as quickly and steadily as you can. And keep your eyes on the road.

4. **Look for a safe place to guide your vehicle** onto the shoulder of the road or some other safe location. In an emergency, the quicker you think and act, the safer you'll be.

Your Accelerator Sticks

1. **Try pulling it up with the toe of your shoe.** If a passenger is with you, have him reach down and pull it up. **You should not take your eyes off the road to reach down yourself.**

2. **If your car has a manual transmission,** press down on the clutch. The engine will continue to race, but you can then pull safely off the road.

3. **If it's an automatic transmission,** put it in neutral. It's not a good idea to turn off the key. Some cars will lose power steering or even lock the steering wheel.

Your Hood Flies Open

You need to stop, but if you slam on your brakes, you could be hit from behind.

1. In some cars, from behind the wheel you can actually see ahead by **peeking through the opening between the dashboard and the hood.**

2. If not, then **lean out the window to see what's ahead of you.**

3. In either case, you need to **slow down smoothly and pull off the road.**

Your Car Goes Into Deep Water

While this doesn't happen often, it happens enough that you should know what to do.

1. If you do go in the water, **release your safety belt immediately.** (But don't release it before you go in. The safety belt will help protect you during impact with the water.)

2. Then the best thing to do is to **try to get out quickly through the window,** because power windows can short-circuit in the water.

3. **If you can't get out through the window, try the door.** At first, the water pressure will probably hold it closed. But don't panic. As the water rises, it will equalize the pressure and the door should open.

IN THE NEXT CHAPTER, we provide a Q&A on what you can do if you come upon an accident or if you are in one yourself.

Chapter 25

Crash Course:

Simple Tips that Could Help Save Lives[1]

I've just seen a bad collision. What can I do to help?

First and foremost, **don't make things worse.**

1. **Pass well beyond the wreck before signaling and pulling off of the road, out of harm's way.** This keeps you from blocking the view of the collision to oncoming traffic, and it gives emergency crews room to work.

2. **Turn on your emergency flashers and raise your hood** to call attention to yourself.

3. Then **carefully approach the wreck, avoiding dangerous situations** like wires, fires or hazardous materials.

4. Next, **turn off the ignitions of all vehicles to reduce the risk of fire.** This simple step could keep a bad collision from becoming much worse. Remember, check for spilled gasoline or downed power lines before getting too close. And don't move an injured driver to get to his keys.

---

[1] Copyright Shell Oil Company material reproduced with permission. Written in cooperation with the National Safety Council and the American Trauma Society.

NOTE: Contains general recommendations that we believe will be helpful in many emergencies. Since every emergency is different, the individual driver must decide what to do in any particular case.

6. Now **call for help if possible.** Be sure to stay on the line until the emergency dispatcher hangs up. If you're needed to administer first aid, assign the call to someone else and be specific: "You in the red jacket call 9-1-l!"

7. **Consider carrying a cellular phone in your car**. Many of today's models have emergency numbers programmed into them.

8. **Check for injuries.** Are victims awake and responsive? If so, encourage them not to move. If they don't respond, verify that they are breathing. Then attend to those with severe bleeding (wear latex gloves if possible).

> **Remember: NEVER MOVE A VICTIM UNLESS THERE IS AN IMMEDIATE, LIFE-THREATENING DANGER SUCH AS FIRE, LEAKING FUEL, OR RISING WATER.**

Should I always stop?

Whatever the situation, your intervention might help save a life.

- **Wouldn't *you* want to be helped** if you were the one trapped or injured?

- Also, **if you were involved in the collision, you *must* stop.** All states impose severe penalties on drivers who don't stop in such cases. **Remember, you can be "involved" in a collision without actually hitting anything.** If you contribute to a crash in any way, you're *obligated* to stop.

- If the fear of making a mistake keeps you from stopping, **be aware that most states have "Good Samaritan" laws to protect individuals from liability** if they stop and, in good faith, administer first aid. The scope of protection varies, so check your state's laws.

IF EMERGENCY CREWS ARE RACING TO A CRASH AHEAD OF YOU, pull over to let them safely pass. And don't assume the first ambulance or police car you see will be the only one. Watch for other emergency vehicles following closely behind the first. The last thing you want to do is pull out and cause another collision.

What's my first step in treating the injured?

- Before beginning any first aid, **check to see if any victims are awake and responsive**. This may help you assess the level of care each victim needs.

- **A conscious victim's responses will often help you evaluate the extent of his injuries.** "What hurts?" may reveal broken bones, bleeding or internal injuries. "Can you wiggle your fingers or toes?" could help you assess potential spinal damage. And no response at all might mean a victim isn't breathing.

I don't think she's breathing! Now what?

1. First, **make sure breathing has stopped.** Is the victim completely non-responsive? Is her chest rising and failing? Can you feel breathing? Hear it? If the victim is not breathing, open her airway. Gently move the head into its normal, "eyes front" position and lower the jaw.

2. **Listen for gurgling or gagging.** Both are signs of a blocked airway. If you hear either after opening the mouth, gently clear it of any obstructions.

3. **If the victim is still not breathing, begin artificial respiration.** Pinch the victim's nose shut. Open your mouth wide, take a deep breath, and put your mouth tightly over the victim's (you may wish to carry a pocket mask or mouth barrier for such emergencies). Blow a full breath, then watch for the

victim's chest to rise and fall. If she doesn't start
breathing on her own, blow one full breath every five
seconds. Do this for at least one minute. Be sure to
breathe yourself — you don't want to hyperventilate!

How do I control severe bleeding.

1. **Press firmly against any wounds with some sort
   of bandage,** preferably a thick pad of clean cloth. This
   will absorb the blood and allow it to clot. (If possible,
   place a barrier — several layers of cloth, latex gloves, a
   plastic bag — between you and the victim's blood.)

2. **If blood soaks through the dressing, don't
   remove it.** That could open the wound further make
   bleeding worse. Instead, **add more layers of cloth
   and apply pressure even more firmly.** If possible,
   get someone else at the scene to help you tie the
   bandage in place.

3. **If the bleeding still won't stop' make sure
   you're pressing on the right spot.** It's *not* a good
   idea to use your belt as a tourniquet. That might
   completely cut off the flow of blood, and could
   potentially lead to the loss of the limb.

All this blood and breathing. Should I be worried about AIDS?

It's a common question, with a comforting answer.

- According to the American Medical Association, **it is
  "extremely unlikely" that you will contract
  AIDS from a bleeding collision victim, or from
  mouth-to-mouth contact during artificial
  respiration.**

- **The HIV virus,** which causes AIDS, **is transmitted
  through sexual contact, infected blood,
  infected needles or childbirth,** and not through
  casual contact.

- Still, for added peace of mind, **you may want to keep several pairs of latex gloves in your first aid kit** (freezer bags are a good substitute).

If I have to move someone, how should I do it?

Remember, you should only move a crash victim when there is an immediate danger, such as fire or rising water.

- **If you must move a victim, gently align his neck and spine.** Then, if you are alone, carefully drag him backward by the clothes or armpits. **Do not pull a victim sideways,** as this will only aggravate spinal damage.

- **If you have help available,** have one person support the head from underneath, keeping it in line with the spine. The others can then lift the body from the sides, evenly supporting it from underneath.

I think she's in shock. Now what?

Shock occurs when a victim's circulatory system doesn't provide enough blood to his body and brain.

- **A person doesn't have to appear injured to suffer from shock** — in fact, shock victims often walk, talk and at first seem merely "shaken up." **Shock can kill, so know how to recognize it.**

- **Telltale signs** include pale, moist, clammy skin; dilated pupils; a weak and rapid pulse; shivering; thirst; nausea and vomiting; shallow breathing; weakness; a vacant expression and a detached attitude.

- **If you suspect an apparently uninjured victim is in shock, have her lie down and raise her feet slightly.**

- It's generally best to **place blankets and coats under her and around her to conserve heat.**

- **If the victim is nauseated,** have her lie on her side and slightly elevate her head.

- **Then begin any additional first aid, talking to the victim as you work.** A little kindness and understanding go a long way toward treating shock

How can I help myself if I'm in a wreck?

- **If it's a minor collision with no injuries,** you can best help yourself by staying calm and moving out of traffic. The key here is safety first, insurance later. Keep a pad and pencil handy, and use them, along with insurance forms, to exchange information once you've cleared the scene.

- **If you're in a major collision,** you'll have to be the judge of whether or not you are injured and how quickly traffic is moving around you. Often, your best bet is to wait for help from a safe place — which just might be your car. If you're uninjured and traffic permits, you may want to begin first aid on those around you. But don't put yourself at more risk doing so. You'll be no help to anyone if you lapse into shock or get struck by a passing motorist.

> **See Ch. 11, *The Glove Compartment and Trunk: Keep Them Well Stocked for Safety* for tips and some warnings and cautionary notes on what to have on hand for roadside emergencies.**

PART IV

DRIVING IN
SPECIAL
SITUATIONS

In this Part, we look at strategies and techniques for driving in situations that pose special hazards — driving in foul weather of all types, driving at night, roadside breakdowns, road rage, and driving alone.

250

Chapter 26
Driving

Foul Weather Driving[1]

Along with coping with the variables of road design, drivers must also cope with weather-related road conditions. Whether it's light rain or heavy snow, high winds or extreme heat, knowing how to adjust your driving and what car safety gear to have with you can mean the difference between being safe or becoming a statistic.

DRIVING IN RAIN

While driving in rain isn't quite as traumatic as driving in snow or ice, it has terrors of its own. Wet weather of any kind demands a gentle touch with vehicle controls. Rain lowers visibility, and creates the need for longer stopping distance, and increases the risks of losing control, especially after radical control movements.

When it rains can be as important as *how much* it rains. If rains fall after a long dry spell, the road will be far more slippery than if it has been raining regularly for several days. In Florida and other southern states, they refer to this

---

[1] Sections in this chapter marked with * are copyright Shell Oil Company materials, used with permission.

road condition as **"black ice."** The initial rainfall floats off all the surface oil the road has collected from cars, forming a very slippery suspension that eventually washes away as the rain continues, especially if it rains long or hard enough. (But then all that water itself becomes a problem.) **A merely wet surface can be tricky; an oily wet surface can be deadly.**

When driving in rain, **here are some simple rules to follow:**

- **Drive slower than usual.** Bear in mind that you do not have the vehicular control you usually do.

- **Turn on your headlights** if it is raining. This allows other drivers to see you and is the law in some states.

- Of course, you must **turn on you windshield wipers**. Make sure they're always in good working order. Don't wait for the next cloudburst to find out your wipers don't work, or that the blades are worn to point of uselessness. (See tips on routine wiper care, p. 37)

- **Make sure your outside mirrors and rear window are clear.** If they are covered with water beads, your view can be distorted, or it can be just plain difficult to see.

- **Don't change speed or direction quickly, and don't brake suddenly.** This is a sure way of encountering a potentially disastrous skid.

- **On a multi-lane highway, stay in the middle lanes.** Water usually collects in the outside lanes.

- **Never drive through large pools of water.** They may be deeper than you think.

Hydroplaning*

Hydroplaning occurs when a thin layer of water causes your tires to lose contact with the road. It can happen even at relatively low speeds and, in the blink of an eye, you can lose control of your car. It's frightening, but don't panic.

- **Keep both hands on the steering wheel.**

- **Ease foot *off* the accelerator.**

- ***Don't* slam on the brakes.**

- ***Without* anti-lock brakes (ABS)**, if wheels lock-up and you begin to skid, simply release the brake pedal then gently re-apply pressure. Steer gently in the direction you want the car to go. (Check your owner's manual to see if you have ABS.)

To avoid hydroplaning:

- Slow down in wet weather.

- Be sure your tires have plenty of tread, and proper inflation. Consider getting "all weather" tires that are specially designed for bad conditions.

When Rain Causes a Flood or There Is Rushing Water*

Always take flood warnings seriously.

> **Do not drive through standing water and *never* drive through rushing water.**

- Water may be very deep in a flooded area and **undercurrents can sweep away even the heaviest vehicles.**

- Watch fences, trees and buildings on the side of the road. **If they appear unnaturally low, slow down immediately.** The road is probably dangerously flooded.

- **Driving into floodwater at high speed is like hitting a wall.**

If Your Vehicle Stalls in Water*

If your vehicle stalls, **abandon it and immediately seek higher ground.**

> **Six inches of rapidly moving floodwater can sweep you off your feet, and two feet of water can carry away the average car.**

DRIVING IN SNOW

Driving in snow can be a white knuckle experience for even the most experienced drivers. The best advice for driving in snow is DON'T. Unless, of course, you drive in an emergency capacity and your job demands it. If you must go out in snow, however, there *are* some things you can do to make life a little easier and safer.  And, if possible, wait until the roads have been plowed before heading out.

Prepare to Get Under Way

- First, **make sure you can see.** Clean all snow from all car windows and mirrors. Don't play *Tank Commander* and just clear a little slit for you to look through.

- *Remember:* **using wipers on an icy windshield can cut wipers to shreds.**

- **Don't drive wearing boots so big they interfere with pedal operation** — a boot so wide that it depresses the brake pedal when you think your foot is only on the gas. This may sound like a ludicrous recommendation but it's surprising how many folks do this.

- Once you've got proper boots on, **make sure to keep them clear of clumps of ice or snow that could interfere with pedal use.** Snow or ice on the soles of boots can cause them to slide off pedals at critical times.

Maintaining Traction on Snow*

To help maintain traction as you are getting underway:

- **Automatic transmission:** Put your car in "D2" and accelerate gently. Shift to "D" once you're moving.

- **Standard transmission:** Use the highest gear, such as 2nd or 3rd, with which you can move the car without stalling.

- Accelerate gently.

As you are driving in snow:

- Slow down.

- Avoid sudden maneuvers.

- Try to keep moving and keep your wheels from spinning, no matter how slow you must go to do so. Use tire chains where allowed by law.

- When driving downhill, use a low gear and let the engine help you keep the car in control.

If you begin to slide:

- Don't slam on the brakes.

- Simply *ease* off the accelerator, then gently apply brake pressure and steer in the direction you want the car to go.

- Be ready to correct for a slide in the opposite direction.

Remember that overpasses and bridges freeze before other pavement. Even if it seems warm enough for ice to melt, it still can be hazardous.

If You Get Stuck in Snow or Ice

- **Apply a traction aid such as sand or kitty litter to the surface under the tire.**

- **Briefly rock the vehicle.**

- **Avoid spinning the wheels.**

   Spinning the tires doesn't get the car free. Spinning the tires only makes the road surface slicker by melting snow which then refreezes as ice, and also creates ruts that can further complicate the process of freeing the car.

   The increased tire speed is not going to create traction. Peak traction is generated at very low speeds. Once a tire is spinning 15 percent faster than the car is moving, maximum traction has been lost.

As you accelerate to get unstuck, do not exceed 35 mph *speedometer* speed — and make sure *no one* stands near the spinning tire.

- When all else fails, **have the vehicle towed**.

BLIZZARD CONDITIONS*

If you become trapped during a blizzard, DO NOT leave the car unless help is visible within 100 yards.

- It is easy to become **disoriented and lost** in blowing, drifting snow and white-out conditions.

- If you live in an area where heavy snow is a problem, **always carry a cell phone and call for help** as soon as you become stuck.

- **Tie a bright-colored cloth to your antenna; raise the hood.**

- Start the engine, turn on the interior light and heater for about **10 minutes each hour.**

- **Beware of carbon monoxide poisoning.** Keep the exhaust pipe clear. Slightly open a downwind window as a vent.

- **Watch for signs of frostbite and hypothermia.** Clap your hands and move your legs to stimulate circulation.

- Use maps, newspaper or car mats for more **insulation.**

Driving in snow and ice is a serious matter, and winter storms can strand drivers for hours before help can arrive. Being prepared could save your life.

- Stock your vehicle with **extra gloves, hats, blankets, a windshield scraper and thermal packs.**

- Also carry **sand, salt or calcium chloride.**

- If you don't have **snow tires**, carry **tire chains.** Practice putting on the tire chains so you know how to use them.

DRIVING ON ICE

One of the most frightening experiences in driving is suddenly going from a dry road surface to one that's covered with ice. The experience is analogous to running at full speed and then abruptly discovering you are running on ice. You look like something out of a children's cartoon — your feet are windmilling like mad while your body stays put. Eventually, your feet will shoot out from under you and down you'll come.

All this pretty much holds true for a car on an icy surface. Under dry conditions, your *feet* are like little car tires. *Real* car tires grab the surface and propel the car forward. Imagine a car on a dry surface approaching ice. The rear wheels are propelling the car, while the front wheels are steering the vehicle (obviously, on front-wheel drive vehicles, the front wheels are performing both these vital functions). **Suddenly, the car encounters ice and none of the tires have any adhesion whatsoever;** absolutely no propulsive or directional control.

And, as if this weren't bad enough, **it all happens instantly.** A rapid transition from dry pavement to ice can cause a driver to over-react, or react roughly with the car's controls, throwing the vehicle completely out of control.

The first and most obvious solution to ice driving is to slow down. But **the steering or braking you are now contemplating will have to be done as *delicately* as possible,** because nearly any control input on ice will result in the vehicle going wildly, completely, utterly out of control.

Stopping and Braking on Ice

When encountering ice or icy conditions and you need to stop, or you find you have to brake and turn:

- **With non-ABS brakes,** first apply brakes as lightly as possible. Then release the brakes and steer, again, gently.

- **With ABS (anti-lock brakes)**, maintain light pressure and steer in the direction you wish to go.

- **Do not try to stop the car by shifting into a lower gear.** When you shift into low gear, the rear wheels can spin and the car will begin to travel sideways. And one of the reasons you are in trouble on ice in the first place is because your wheels are spinning and not creating any traction on a slippery surface. If you put the car in a lower gear, the rear tires spin faster, making the situation worse, not better.

> **REMEMBER: Stopping on snow and ice may require up to 10 times the distance as stopping in normal conditions. Keep plenty of distance between you and the vehicle in front of you.**

To Recover from an Ice Slide

If you do hit the ice and begin to slide:

- Put the car in **neutral.**

- **Then press *gently* on the brake pedal.** *You must be gentle.* Do not brake abruptly — over-applying the brakes will only increase the trouble you're already in.

- **Steer in the direction you want the car to go**. You MUST use a light touch on the controls here. Be careful how much you turn the steering wheel. If you turn it too much and over correct, the car will begin to fishtail.

- **Once you have straightened out, apply a very slight amount of gas.**

WINTER DRIVING SCENARIO — THE DYNAMICS IN "ACTION"

The following is a scenario familiar to those that have had the chance to drive on ice:

You cruise around the corner of Main and Elm. **It's winter, but today is nice and sunny, but cold.** You approach the corner at 40 mph, slowing to 20 mph and turn the wheel approximately 45 degrees. You round the corner successfully and five seconds later, you've forgotten the entire, routine maneuver.

The next day, the temperature has dropped twenty degrees and it's snowing heavily. The road is very slippery. You approach the same corner at 40 mph, and attempt to slow to 20 mph. The first sign of trouble comes when you try to slow. Not much happens when you apply the brakes. The car is still traveling forward, a little slower than before, but still traveling. Because of the slippery surface, there is no friction to stop the car.

You turn the steering wheel to the same 45 degrees that worked just fine yesterday. Only this time nothing happens. The car continues traveling in a straight line.

What are the dynamics of what worked yesterday and what isn't working today? On yesterday's dry pavement, the tires had sufficient adhesion to propel, control, and stop the car. Today, on a slick surface, they don't.

So the *techniques* for vehicle control are different as well. Today you must lower the forces involved. How is that done? Remove the source of the force; the vehicle's speed, and the angle of the turn. Now, we'll be the first to admit that it is rather difficult to drive around a corner without turning the wheel. So that leaves us with but a single answer: SLOW

DOWN! That's it. It's so simple. If the weather has altered the road conditions: SLOW DOWN.

> **Wet roads are at their slipperiest when the temperature is near freezing. Solidly frozen ice is the most dangerous. Snow provides better traction than ice if it is not too packed and there's no ice under it.**

If you are an emergency worker, slowing down is tough to do when you're trying to get to people in trouble. But those people you're trying to reach in such a hurry are depending on your help, and you can't give them that help if you crack up your valuable rescue vehicle and yourself on the way to them.

FOG*

When it comes to inclement weather, fog is one of the most visually limiting conditions. If you get caught in heavy fog, the best thing to do is to stop well off the road until visibility is better. **If there is no safe place to stop:**

- Take all fog-related warning signs seriously.

- **Slow down.** Fog makes it very difficult to judge speed. Do not believe your eyes — **glance at your speedometer to make sure you have slowed down.**

- **Turn on wipers, defroster and low-beam headlights.** Using high beams can actually decrease your visibility.

- Moisture from fog can make roads slick, so **brake smoothly.**

- **Crack your window and turn off the radio**. Watch for slower moving cars and listen for engine sounds or car horns.

- **If the fog is too dense to continue,** pull completely off the road and try to position your vehicle in a protected area from other traffic. **Turn on your emergency flashers.**

- Consider installing **"fog lights"** if you often drive in fog.

EXTREME HEAT*

Sunscreen and insect repellent are important in the summer, but so is a quick vehicle inspection before heading out to a favorite recreation spot. **During hotter months, it's a good idea to keep extra coolant, at least one gallon of water, jumper cables and a flashlight in your vehicle.** Also:

- Check the battery, belts and hoses.

- Check oil often.

- Have your air-conditioning system checked and serviced by a qualified technician.

- Inspect your coolant and water level and ratio to be sure it is at the proper 50/50 level when the car is cool.

- Never leave children or pets unattended in a car even for a short time. The temperature inside a closed vehicle — even with windows down — can reach dangerous levels very quickly.

- Cover metal and plastic parts on child seats and safety belts to prevent burns.

What to Do If Your Car Overheats

- **Let engine cool and call for service.**

- If your engine overheated because of **lack of coolant,** further operation may damage the vehicle.

LIGHTNING*

With or without accompanying rain, lightning can be dangerous.

- **If you're in your car during a lightning storm,** DO NOT attempt to leave the vehicle and run for cover. The car's metal cage will conduct a charge into the ground and protect you.

- If you're in an open vehicle, such as a convertible, golf cart, tractor, motorcycle or bicycle, find safe shelter.

- **Do not stand under trees or in small, isolated buildings** because lightning will usually strike the tallest object around. Instead, **crouch down on the balls of your feet.**

Chapter 27

Driving Safely at Night:

There's More to It Than Good Headlights

Most drivers think the only difference between day and night driving is that one requires headlights. True, most of the light we have available for our use at night comes from our car's headlights — but **headlights are a poor substitute for daylight.**

Compound this with the fact that even during daylight, safe driving depends not only on **as far as you can see,** but on **how much you can see,** and **how fast you can see it and react to it.** And we know that after the sun goes down, all these factors change *dramatically.*

So, what can you do **to *minimize* the hazards of driving at night.** Here are some tips.

Keep Your Headlights in Good Working Order

Good night visibility is more than just *having* headlights; you must keep them in optimum condition.

- **Make sure your headlights are aligned properly.** You can have the best headlight system in the world, but if those lights point off in crazy directions, they're not going to do much good, except to make your vehicle a kind of traveling light show. Tests can be performed to see if the lights on your car are aligned properly.

- **Keep headlights clean.** As much as half of a headlight's total illumination can be absorbed by dirt on the surface of the glass beam. Keeping headlights clean is especially important in winter when they are frequently covered with road dirt and encrusted with salt.

Keep Your Windshield and Mirrors Clean

The glare through a dirty windshield can make visibility almost nonexistent. The same for mirrors. Keep both the outside and inside of your windshield as clean as possible. And make sure your windshield wipers are in good condition. There's nothing like a smear of bug juice, bird droppings, and road oils on your windshield spread around by worn out wipers to make your night driving an experience to remember. (See p. 37 for tips on how to keep your windshield and wipers in optimum condition.)

Adjust Your Speed to the Range of Your Headlights

Contrary to common sense, **many drivers do not slow down significantly when driving at night** — despite their reduced visibility and the added dangers of inclement weather.

We've all seen this type of driver. *You're* tooling along at a reduced speed at night in a driving rainstorm. The windshield wipers are slapping back and forth at their highest setting when suddenly a pair of headlights appear in your rear-view mirror. These headlights grow bigger and brighter at an alarming rate, and before we know it — zoom! — a car goes flashing past us, apparently oblivious to the darkness, the weather, and the fact that it's hard to see 50 feet ahead of the car on a night like this. This driver is overdriving his headlights and may be headed for disaster!

- **Don't overdrive your headlights.** Never drive so fast that you cannot stop within the distance you can see ahead with your lights.

  High-beam headlights in good working order illuminate the road for about 330 feet ahead; low beams illuminate for about 200 feet ahead.

  If, for example, you're driving with your low beams on and your speed is 40 mph (approximately 60 ft/sec) you have three seconds' worth of vision ahead of you — assuming that your headlights are clean and working at maximum efficiency. (See Figure 17-4, p. 171

- **Establish a safe following distance.** For daylight driving in the average car traveling 40mph or less, the rule of thumb is to keep two-seconds between you and the traffic ahead. For night driving make it a three-second rule. (See p. 170 for tips on figuring out exactly how much space is necessary, especially at higher speeds and for longer vehicles).

Keep Your Eyes Moving

Don't just focus on the middle of the lighted area in front of you. Headlights only illuminate so much and they cannot see around corners.

- **Search the edges of the lighted area.** Look for other patches of light that could be cars. Look for them at hilltops, on curves, or at intersections.

- Where there are many **distracting neon signs or brightly-lit buildings,** try to concentrate on street-level activities.

- **When you turn corners at night,** don't just follow the headlights around the corner. As you turn your car, scan the areas to the side and beyond the headlights.

- **When backing up**, remember that only your backup lights are available; on most makes of cars, they aren't much.

Protect Your Eyes from Glare

Prolonged exposure to glare from sunlight during the day or headlights at night can temporarily ruin your night vision, while also leading to eye strain and drowsiness.

- **Wear good sunglasses on bright days** and take them off as soon as the sun goes down.

- **Rest a while before driving at night after a long session of steady daytime driving.**

- **If the high beams of an oncoming car are not dimmed, avoid looking directly at the bright lights.** When your eyes are hit by a bright beam of light from an oncoming car, you can't see! Drivers can be affected by the oncoming glare of headlights as far as 3,000 feet away. You can be completely blinded for a full one or two seconds, which means that at 40 mph you will drive somewhere from 60 to 120 feet without being able to see anything clearly.

- **Glance toward the right side of the road; then quickly look ahead to determine the other vehicle's position.** Keep doing this until you have passed each other.

- Avoid driving long distances without taking breaks. Continual glare of lights outside and from your dashboard increase the chance of highway hypnosis.

Use Your Lights Wisely

- **Use low beams when driving in cities and towns,** except on streets where there is no other lighting.

- **Use low beams whenever you are following a vehicle.**

- **Use high-beam headlights on highways only when it is safe and legal to do so**, such as when no other vehicle is coming toward you. Switch to low beams when following another car or encountering on-coming cars to avoid blinding the other driver.

Make It Easy for Others to See You

- **Turn on your low beams (not your parking lights) at dusk or dawn.** Used at this time of day, they won't help you see, but they'll help other drivers and pedestrians see you.

- **Some states require you to use headlights from sunset to sunrise.** Most late model cars have automatic "running lights" for daytime driving. If your car doesn't, use your low beams.

- **If you have to pull off the road and stop, for whatever reason, put on your emergency flashers.** It's not a bad idea to turn on the car's interior or dome lights. If the car's electrical system fails, have a combination of flares, a flashlight, and some reflective materials handy.

- **Bright color and high contrast make objects visible at night.** That's why it's a good idea to have some reflecting tape on the outside of your vehicle, especially if the vehicle is a dark color.

Avoid Steady Driving at the Hour of Your Usual Bedtime

- **A person's alertness level decreases around the time one routinely retires for the night.** If you must drive past your usual bedtime, stop every hour or so and walk around. Stretch your legs. Get some air.

And ALWAYS drive *defensively* at night.

Chapter 28

Roadside Breakdown:

How to Deal with Roadside Emergencies[1]

Each year, nearly 3,000 people die in car accidents on the shoulder or median of the road. Sometimes, these fatal scenarios begin with a simple breakdown that forces the vehicle off the roadway. **Learning how to prevent breakdowns and how to protect yourself and your passengers if a breakdown occurs can save your life.**

How do I know something is wrong with my vehicle?

- **Watch the instrument panel.** Your instrument panel gauges indicate engine temperature, fuel and oil levels and other important information. Read your owner's manual to familiarize yourself with all the gauges. Your manual will also indicate what gauge readings are considered "normal" and which signal an emergency situation.

- **However, your instrument panel can't tell you everything.** For example, if your car suddenly pulls to one side, or if you feel a rumbling or vibration,

---

[1] Copyright Shell Oil Company material reproduced with permission. Written in cooperation with the American Red Cross, the Federal Highway Administration, the National Crime Prevention Council, and the National Institute for Automotive Servence Excellence.

NOTE: Contains general recommendations that we believe may be helpful in the event of a breakdown. Because every situation is different, the individual driver must decide what to do in each particular scenario.

safely pull off the roadway. You may have a flat or low tire.

- *Keep alert.* **Your sense of smell, touch, sight or hearing may be the first hint that there's a problem.** Pay attention to your car while driving. An odd odor, an unusual vibration, the sight of smoke or an unexpected sound can signal trouble.

If there's something wrong with my vehicle, should I stop where I am or continue?

It really depends on the nature of your problem.

- As a safe rule of thumb, **any change in your vehicles's steering, braking or acceleration should receive immediate attention.** Pull safely to the side of the road onto a smooth, flat shoulder as far off the roadway as possible.

- On the other hand, with **less urgent problems, such as an underinflated tire, a slight shift in a gauge's reading, or a blown fuse,** it's usually okay to continue cautiously to the closest service station.

If I have to pull over, how do I do it safely?

- **Reduce distractions inside your vehicle** by turning off the stereo and asking passengers, especially children, to remain still and quiet.

- **Gradually reduce speed** and **visually check off-road conditions** before choosing where to pull over.

- **Use your turn signal and not your emergency flashers so other drivers will know you need**

to get over. When your emergency flashers are on, your blinkers don't work.

- Check for traffic and, **when it's clear, move smoothly one lane at a time from the roadway to the shoulder.**

- **Avoid soft shoulders, curbs, uneven areas and curves that will prevent other drivers from seeing you.**

- **Don't jerk the wheel or swerve.** That could cause your tires to "catch" on the side of the road.

- **Even though you are off the roadway, remain extra cautious.** Vehicles on the shoulder or median are still at risk for collisions. After you've stopped, turn on your emergency flashers.

How should I get help?

- Once you're safely off the road, **turn on your emergency flashers.**

- **If you don't have a cellular phone or CB radio, place a sign in the window that says "Call Police."** If you don't have a "Call Police" sign, carry a marker and piece of paper so you can make your own. Many store-bought sunshades have a "Call Police" sign on one side.

- In addition, **use a handkerchief or bright piece of clothing to signal for help.** Attach it to the outside of your car where it can be easily seen, like on an antenna or door handle. If this requires you to exit your vehicle, use the door furthest from the road.

Should I stay in my car while waiting for help?

- Yes. **It's best to stay in your car with the windows up and doors locked** — *unless* there is smoke, the threat of an engine or electrical fire or the possibility of ventilation problems. (See Box 11-1, p. 107 for important cautions and warnings about fire or smoke associated with a vehicle.)

- **Be patient**. Help will arrive.

- **Keep your seat belt fastened while waiting,** in case you're struck by another vehicle.

- **If you experience a breakdown in extreme heat**, keep your windows cracked and drink plenty of water. Always carry emergency drinking water in hot weather.

- **Some repairs may require passengers to exit the vehicle.** For example, no one should be in a vehicle when a tire is being changed.

What if a stranger approaches?

- **Be on guard.** DON'T open the doors or windows to communicate. If the person behaves suspiciously, tell them the police are on their way.

- **If you're offered the use of a cellular phone or CB radio, don't accept.** Instead, write down the number you need to call and show it to the person through the window. (Always keep a message pad and pen in your glove compartment.)

- **If it's absolutely necessary or you feel confident, lower your window just enough to speak through it.** Ask them to call or send for help.

Are there any repairs I can make to get myself moving again?

> **There's so much technology in today's vehicles, many repairs can only be made by certified technicians with the proper diagnostic equipment and tools.**

But there are some minor repairs you may be able to make if you have the right tools and materials.

- For example, **you may be able to change a tire, add oil or coolant, replace a fuse or pour water into the radiator.** (Remember to let your engine cool before removing the radiator cap. The hot water in your radiator is under extreme pressure and can cause severe burns. Be patient, it may take more than an hour to cool.)

What if I get a flat tire?

- ***Don't panic*. Firmly grip the wheel and slowly pull off the road as far as possible.** If you're in an unsafe area or on a busy roadway, don't try to change the tire. Drive slowly to a safer place. This may cause damage to your rim, but isn't it better to risk your rim than risk your life?

How to change a tire the right way

1. After pulling off the road and stopping in a safe place, put the car in park and apply the parking (emergency) brake. If your car has a standard transmission, place the gear shift in reverse or first gear. Park on solid, level ground if possible.

2. Retrieve the spare tire, jack and lug wrench. Remove any hub cap with the lug wrench.

3. Before lifting the car with the jack, first loosen each lug nut one turn counterclockwise while the car is still on the ground. The weight of the car will make this easier.

4. Place the jack under the reinforced section of the car's body. The location of these sections is listed in your owner's manual.

5. Jack up the car until the flat tire is several inches off the ground. WARNING: Never place your hands or feet under the vehicle or tire once it has been raised.

6. Remove the lug nuts and remove the wheel.

7. Place the spare tire on the axle and align the holes. Replace the lug nuts and tighten each lightly.

8. Lower the car, and remove the jack. Then use the wrench to firmly tighten each lug nut.

9. Have the flat tire repaired or replaced and reinstalled right away.

How can I jumpstart a battery safely?

To ensure a safe jump, follow these guidelines and review your owner's manual:

A. Position vehicles so jumper cables can reach, but vehicles ARE NOT TOUCHING.

> **WHEN HOLDING JUMPER CABLES MAKE SURE THE ENDS NEVER TOUCH.**

B. Connect one end of the RED cable to the POSITIVE terminal of the dead battery (1). Connect the other end of the RED cable to the POSITIVE terminal of the good battery (2).

C. Connect one end of the BLACK cable to the NEGATIVE terminal of the good battery (3). Connect the other end of the BLACK cable to an engine bolt head or other piece of non-moving metal (4).

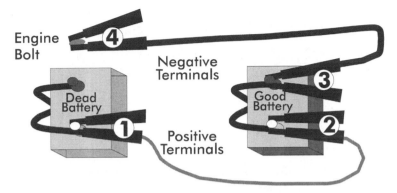

Figure 28-1. Correct Jumper Cable-to-Battery Connections for Jumpstarting a Vehicle.

> **WARNING: ATTACHING THE BLACK CABLE TO THE NEGATIVE TERMINAL OF THE DEAD BATTERY INSTEAD OF AN ENGINE BOLT MAY RESULT IN AN EXPLOSION.**

D. Make sure the jumper cables are away from moving engine parts.

E. Start the engine with the good battery. Run it at moderate speed.

F. Start the engine of the vehicle with the dead battery according to your owner's manual. Once it starts, reduce engine speed to idle.

G. Remove the jumper cables in REVERSE order. First remove the BLACK cable from the engine bolt head or metal connection on the car you jumpstarted.

H. The engine needs to run for at least 30 minutes to start recharging the battery. This can include driving time.

> **Once the car has been jumpstarted, you should have a certified technician test the battery and charging system.**

What can I do to *prevent* a breakdown?

Every time you drive your vehicle, check the following:

- ☑ Tires for proper inflation.
- ☑ Windshield, headlights and taillights should be clean.
- ☑ Survey gauges and warning lights after you have started your car.

As part of *routine maintenance* you should:

- ☑ Check oil level once a week; change the oil every 3,000 miles or as recommended by your owner's manual.
- ☑ Check for oil leaks.
- ☑ Check tires for cuts, nails, stones and proper inflation.
- ☑ Help prevent uneven tire wear; rotate tires every 5,000 to 6,000 miles. Research shows 90% of tire problems occur in the last 10% of a tire's life.
- ☑ Make sure the battery and its terminal are clean and corrosion free.
- ☑ Check the air filter; replace if it's dirty.
- ☑ Check fluid levels for brakes, steering, windshield washer, radiator coolant and automatic transmission.
- ☑ Make sure the exhaust system has no visible leaks or cracks and the tail pipe is not obstructed.
- ☑ Carry only securely stored, non-flammable liquids in the trunk — never gasoline.
- ☑ Before trips, check fluid levels, belts, hoses, and clamps. Refill or replace if necessary.

All procedures should be done in accordance with your owner's manual.

See also: Ch. 9, *Smart Car Care: Tips for Keeping Your Vehicle Safe and on the Road;* Ch. 10, *Know Your Car: The Ten-Minute Check List;* Ch. 11, *The Glove Compartment and Trunk: Keep Them Well Stocked for Safety*

Chapter 29

Road Rage:

How to Avoid It, How to Deal with It

Not like there isn't enough to worry about when we are driving, we now have to cope with **another potentially deadly problem — "Road Rage."**

Anyone who drives on the road these days knows the problem. As you are driving, someone makes an obscene gesture at you, calls you names that are not flattering, questions your parenthood. He may even start tailgating you for long distances, or deliberately cutting you off, or trying to force you off the road. His emotions have gotten the best of him, his anger has boiled over, and he's turned downright aggressive — and ready to risk your life and his. And for what?

What Starts Road Rage?

The American Automobile Association (AAA) indicates that road rage is often started over trivial things — you honked your horn too much, or at all; you took (or wanted to take) a parking space someone else had their eye on. Or maybe you committed the "mortal sin" of slowing someone down, or inadvertently did something that wasn't in the best interest of automotive safety — cut someone off, zigzagged in and out of traffic, or tailgated because *you* were in a hurry — or just not paying attention.

Road Rage often begins with some small gesture

On the other hand, maybe the other driver got behind the wheel *already* enraged by something, and you were just unlucky enough to be on the same road with her at the same time.

> **Whatever the reason, road rage situations can lead to collisions, disputes, even death.**

Who Commits Road Rage?

If you decide to engage a "road rager" in conversation — or worse, decide to play road warrior with him — please understand whom you may be dealing with.

According to the American Automobile Association, **"road ragers" are mostly poorly educated males between the ages of 18 to 26 with criminal records.** They have histories of violence, drug abuse, or alcohol problems, and many have suffered an emotional or professional setback.

Many impatient drivers set themselves up to be victims of road rage. They take risks on the road, which can lead to discourteous driving, which can lead to disputes, which can escalate into road rage.

You may become enraged yourself — "sick and tired" of dealing with aggressive drivers who are "jerks," "idiots," "who don't have all their wagons in a circle," "who have the intelligence quotient of a Styrofoam cup." They can all get you heated up and make you lose your patience, make you do things and take risks you normally wouldn't. They can drag you into their road rage game if you let them. Don't. It can be a *deadly* game.

Things to Do/Don't Do to Avoid or Deal with Road Rage

The general rule is to avoid all conflicts. If another driver wants to get by, let him pass. If she wants a parking space, let her have it. Consider it a contribution to you favorite charity. If another driver challenges you, don't challenge back. Let him go.

Here are some suggestions from the AAA — and then some — on how to avoid and deal with road rage.

- ☑ **DON'T take *traffic problems* personally.** Believe it or not, traffic is not an organized conspiracy to prevent you from being on time.

- ☑ **DO give *yourself* enough time to get where you are going.**

- ☑ **DON'T automatically assume other drivers' *mistakes* are purposely aimed at you.**

- ☑ **If a driver has done something stupid to you — or simply made a mistake, DON'T return the favor.** In other words, don't have a contest to see who is the dumbest — you may just win.

- ☑ **AVOID eye contact with aggressive drivers;** it only encourages them.

- ☑ **If an aggressive driver makes an obscene gesture, DON'T make one or two back at him.** Although it may be incredibly gratifying, it brings you to his level, and can escalate the situation.

- ☑ **If an aggressive driver pursues you, DO find the nearest police station.**

- ☑ **BE CAREFUL about using your horn as a method of communicating** — even a friendly honk can be misinterpreted. **DON'T honk excessively.**

- ☑ **DON'T use high-beam headlights unnecessarily.**

- ☑ **If you drive *slowly,* DO pull over** and let people pass you.

Photo © Eli Haber, 2007
www.imagesbyeli.com

- ☑ **DON'T block the passing lane** — no matter how fast you are going, there will always be someone who wants to go faster.

- ☑ **DON'T switch lanes without signaling first.**

- ☑ **AVOID blocking the right hand turn lane**.

- ☑ **DON'T tailgate**.

- ☑ **DON'T take up more than one parking place.**

- ☑ **DON'T allow your door to hit the car next to you when exiting your car in a parking lot.**

- ☑ **DON'T inflict your loud music on nearby cars.**

REMEMBER: Always be polite and courteous on the road, even if another driver is acting like an idiot.

Chapter 30

Alone Behind the Wheel[1]

Two violent crimes are committed in the U.S. every minute of every day. Drivers traveling alone can be particularly vulnerable. There are a number of things you can do, however, to keep yourself safe. Both inside your car and out. Read about those things here, then pass the information along to anyone who might be alone behind the wheel.

What should I know about parking safety?

Lots. **Where and how you choose to park can go a long way toward keeping you safer.**

- **When possible, *back into* a parking space.** Should you need to, you'll be able to drive out with less chance of someone trapping you.

- **Try to park close to the building entrance.** This will reduce the time you're alone outside your car.

- **If you know you're going to be working late,** move your car to a well-lighted area closer to the exit. Such a precaution may reduce your risk at night.

---

[1] Copyright Shell Oil Company material reproduced with permission. Written in cooperation with the National Crime Prevention Council and the National Safety Council.

NOTE: Contains general recommendations that we believe to be helpful; however, every emergency is different. The individual driver must decide what to do in any particular case.

- **If you're in a parking lot,** always choose a spot that will be well-lighted and away from shrubs and bushes so you can see under and around your car as you approach it.

Should I do anything special in parking garages?

Yes.

- **Park in a well-lighted spot, ground level if available,** close to the parking attendant station.

- If you can't do that, try to **park close to the elevators or stairwell near the building entrance.**

- **Spend as little time as possible going to and from your car**.

- Try to **stay where you can be seen by others** because there's safety in numbers.

- **If you have any concerns at all,** call the building's security service and have someone accompany you to your car.

If I lock my car before I leave it, is that enough?

No. You should take **additional precautions.**

- **If you have a two-door car,** flip your passenger seat forward when you're leaving your vehicle.

- **If it's a four-door car,** move the driver seat forward.

- **Upon your return,** if you see that it has been returned to its original position, go back to the building you came from immediately and notify security of the

police. Someone could be hiding on the back
floorboard.

- **As you approach your car,** don't just look around
  it; look *under* it as well. Criminals sometimes hide
  there.

I hear a lot about carjackings. Is there any way to avoid them?

The FBI estimates that **approximately 25,000 car-
jackings occur in the U.S. each year.** There are
defensive techniques you can use that might keep you
from becoming a carjacking victim.

- **Always keep your doors locked.**

- **Always scan ahead and behind as you drive.**
  Look for individuals who may be loitering near an
  intersection.

- **If it looks as if you may be driving into a
  potentially dangerous situation at an
  upcoming intersection,** slow down and, if you can
  do so safely, time the light to avoid stopping. Be sure
  there is no cross traffic that could cause a collision.

- **Try to keep escape routes open.** Stop far enough
  behind the car in front of you so that you can see its
  back tires touching the pavement. That way, if you
  have to pull out quickly, you won't have to back up
  first. Also, stay in the left-hand land when approaching
  an intersection.

- **What's that "bump and run" carjacking
  thing?** It's a technique carjackers often employ.
  People in one car pull up behind an unsuspecting
  driver and bump that driver's car. When the driver gets
  out to inspect the damage, the carjackers forcibly take
  control of the car and the driver. If you believe that
  you've been intentionally bumped, don't stop and get

out of the car. Drive to a safe, public place close by to check the damage. You'll be a lot less vulnerable.

Got any safety "trip tips"?

- **DO plan your trip before you leave.** Mark your route (how you're going and where you plan to stop) on a map. Give a copy of that plan (with appropriate phone numbers where you can be reached and an estimated time of arrival) to a family member, friend, or business associate.

- **DON'T take maps or other obvious travel aids into rest stops or restaurants.** You don't want to call attention to the fact that you have a long way to travel.

Box 30-1. Your Keychain: Potential Crime Prevention in the Palm of Your Hand

- **Have your keys ready as you approach your vehicle.** Fumbling to find them and unlocking your car takes time and makes you more vulnerable.

- **A small flashlight on your keychain** lets you see your door locks and ignition easier at night. Quicker starts. Quicker getaway.

- **Pepper spray or mace can be attached to your keychain** so you don't have to fumble for it if you ever need it. But be aware that depending on wind direction, spray could blow back in your face. It also could be taken and used against you.

- Sometimes you have to give your keys to others, such as when you valet park. **Keychains that let you easily separate your car keys from your home keys** keep individuals from gaining access to your home.

- **DO check your car out completely before you get on the road.** Many breakdowns are avoidable, especially those involving fuel, oil, cooling or electrical problems.

- **DON'T think just because you have a cellular phone that you won't need to use a public one.** Carry change just in case.

- **DO use valet parking at hotels and restaurants.** It's safer than spending too much time in the parking lots.

- **DON'T try to fix a flat if you think you are in an unsafe area.** Drive slowly to a service station or police station.

Should I always have my door locked when I'm driving?

Yes. All your doors. And you should always have your windows rolled up. If it's hot and you don't have air conditioning, roll your windows down just enough to allow air to flow in, but not enough to allow someone to get his hand in the car.

What do I do if my car just conks out?

- **If your car comes to a stop slowly,** try to pull safely off the road, out of the way of traffic.

- **Stay in your car.**

- **If you have a cell phone, call for help and give them your location.** If you don't have a roadside assistance service, call the police.

- **If you don't have a cell phone, stick a white handkerchief or scarf part way out your**

window. This will alert passers-by that you need assistance.

- **If someone does stop to help you,** stay inside your car with all the doors locked and the windows rolled up high enough so no one can get a hand inside the car. Tell them what kind of help you need. If their concern is genuine, they'll make a call for you or alert someone who can help you at their next stop.

- **Don't get out and raise the hood of your car.** This blocks your view of oncoming traffic (one of whom may be a policeman), and it signals the potential criminal that your car is immobile.

- **You should always carry a "Call Police" window sign in your glove compartment** (or have paper and marker to make one). That way many drivers will see that you need help, and if someone does stop that you are suspicious of, you can tell him that someone saw your sign and has already contacted the police, who are currently en route.

Is Having a phone in the car a good idea?

Yes. But it can be dangerous if not used properly. People using a phone while driving run a 34% higher risk of having a collision.

> **NOTE: Several cities and areas have adopted a "no cell phone use while driving" ordinance.**

- If you must dial, **pull safely off the road, stop, then dial.**

- **Headset or speaker phone units** that allow you to talk and listen without holding a receiver are better, but they can still be dangerous if they pull your attention away from the road.

- If you **preprogram your phone to activate 9-1-1 or other emergency numbers,** you'll be able to react much more quickly in an emergency.

- It's best to **use the phone in the car only as an emergency aid or to let people at your destination know in advance if you are going to be late.** That's better than trying to drive too fast to get there on time.

I seem to get more tired when I drive alone. What can I do about it?

Driver fatigue can be a killer. It's especially dangerous when you are alone. Here are some things you can do to help stay awake:

- **Don't start a trip late in the day**. Get plenty of sleep before you drive.

- **Avoid long drives at night.** The glare of lights outside and from your dashboard increases the chance of highway hypnosis.

- **Adust your car's environment to help you stay awake.** Keep the temperature cool. Don't use cruise control. Keep your body involved in the drive.

- **Use good posture.** Keep your head up, shoulders back, buttocks tucked against the seat back, legs *not* fully extended.

- **Take frequent breaks.** Stop at well-lighted rest areas or service stations, and get out of the car to stretch or have a snack.

- **Avoid alcohol entirely.**

- **Don't allow your eyes to become fatigued.** Wear sunglasses to fight glare during the day.

- **Break the monotony.** Vary your speed levels. Chew gum. Talk to yourself.

- **If you absolutely cannot keep your eyes open,** the best remedy is to **stop and get some sleep.** Staying at a motel for the night is usually the safest bet. If you cannot find a motel, it is still better to be off the road than to fall asleep while driving. If you do pull off the road to take a quick nap, be sure you are *safely* off the road, preferably at a well-lighted, secure rest area, service plaza or truck stop, with all doors locked. If a security guard is present, ask him or her to keep an eye on your car while you're napping.

What if I plan and prepare but someone confronts me anyway?

Your foremost concern should be your personal safety.

- **If you are confronted by a robber or a carjacker, don't resist.** Give up your purse, your wallet and your keys quickly. Do not attempt to reason with a robber. Try to remember what the individual looks like. Remember, possessions can be replaced. Your life can't be.

PART V

RESOURCES

This Part provides an annotated list of selected driving-related websites — some focused exclusively on special driving topics, others broader in focus, but with special-interest forums or sections related to driving or motor vehicles.

You'll find sites with a wealth of driving tips for *everyone* (including new drivers, teenage drivers, older drivers), sites on motor vehicle safety and vehicle crashworthiness, on car maintenance, on buying and selling a car, on RVs, SUVs, even on road safety overseas and driving abroad.

Although far from comprehensive, the list is designed to give you a feel for the broad range of driving-related information available on the Web. Check out the sites, follow their links, type "driver education," "driving techniques," or some specific driving/vehicle-related topic into a search engine or two — and discover the vast resources that await to fill your every driving-information need.

Website Resources

Author's Website

🚗 **Tony Scotti** Offers a wealth of information about both the security industry and driver education. **Website:** SecurityDriver.com

Driving Information Websites

🚗 **Drivers.com** "The world's leading site on drivers and driving." PDE Publications Inc. specializes in driving, driver behavior, and traffic safety, and its website is an information resource for both traffic safety professionals and the general public, with a *wealth* of information on driver training, education, and licensing. Includes special sections for new drivers and older drivers. **Website:** www.drivers.com

🚗 **Seniordrivers.org** (a site of the AAA Foundation for Traffic Safety) Offers tips to help seniors (or any drivers) keep their driving skills sharp. Includes video clips covering some of the trickiest situations drivers might encounter. Also offers information on transportation alternatives for seniors. **Website:** www.seniordrivers.org

🚗 **American Association of Retired Persons (AARP)** Search under "driving" for a *host* of articles on driving-related information and issues and a description of the AARP Driver Safety Program. Many automobile insurers offer discounts to drivers over age 50 who complete the AARP Driver Safety program. The course is the nation's first and largest classroom driver refresher course specially designed for motorists age 50 and older. It is intended to help older drivers improve their skills while teaching them to avoid accidents and traffic violations. The site also offers many safety tips. **Website:** www.aarp.org

ABS Educational Alliance Focuses specifically on anti-lock brakes and driving concerns. Offers a number of educational resources, including online and print brochures on tips for driving with ABS and do's and don't's; driving with intelligent stability and handling systems; ABS videos (viewable online); and ABS curriculum materials for instructors. **Website**: www.abs-education.org

U.S. Department of State Features a section on *Road Safety Overseas* with articles and related links. Covers road safety, road security, international driving permits, tips on driving abroad, auto insurance, treaties on roads and transport, etc. **Website:** travel.state.gov/road_safety.html

Enjoy the Drive "Customize your vehicle for the way you live." This educational consumer website from SEMA (Specialty Equipment Market Association) is about improving vehicles after they have left the factory. For example, custom auto products can help parents make their family vehicle safer; they can help outdoor enthusiasts stow or tow their gear more safely and easily; can help commuters reduce stress and stay more comfortable while on the road, etc. Features a searchable database of accessories, and offers links to the companies that manufacture, sell, and install them. Offers a host of other driving-related features as well. A search for "driving" produces a wealth of driving tips. "Whether you want to learn how to choose the correct tires for your driving purposes, how to tow safely, or how to throw the ultimate tailgate party," this site has the info you need. **Website:** www.enjoythedrive.com

RV Alliance America (RVAA) "The RV Insurance Specialist" is committed to seeing safe RVers on the road.

Features a wealth of information pertaining to driving an RV (but also applicable to driving in general), including RV driving safety, RV insurance issues, fire and life safety, medical emergencies while traveling, accidents (includes a Medical Information Worksheet for travelers), the unique needs of bus conversion owners (including one woman's perspective on driving a coach), how to share the road with truckers, and much more. **Website:** www.rvaa.com

Vehicle/Highway Safety Websites

Crashes and crashtesting

- **Crashtest.com** Provides international crash-test results, insurance ratings, and auto safety information. **Website:** www.crashtest.com

- **National Crash Analysis Center** is a federally-funded research center concentrating on vehicle crashworthiness research. **Website:** www.ncac.gwu.edu

- **Insurance Institute for Highway Safety (IIHS) and Highway Loss Data Institute (HDLI)** A non-profit research and communications organization funded by auto insurers. A leader on finding out what works and doesn't work to prevent motor vehicle crashes in the first place and reducing injuries in the crashes that still occur. Research focuses on countermeasures aimed at all three factors in motor vehicle crashes (human, vehicular, and environmental), and on interventions that can occur before, during, and after crashes to reduce losses. Find data on crashworthy evaluations, air bags, fatalities and other motor vehicle safety topics. Includes vehicle ratings, educational videos, tips for young and older drivers, and FAQs. **Website:** www.carsafety.org

Vehicle, highway, and traffic safety

National Highway Traffic Safety Administration (NHTSA) NHTSA is responsible for reducing deaths, injuries, and economic losses from motor vehicle crashes. This detailed site offers data on its task of setting and enforcing motor-vehicle safety performance standards, and features an exceptionally broad range of special topic articles focusing on vehicle and equipment information and on traffic safety/occupant issues. (Click on the site's Table of Contents for the complete list.) **Website:** www.nhtsa.dot.gov

AAA Foundation for Traffic Safety This highly regarded foundation sponsors research that identifies critical traffic safety problems, searches for underlying causes, and advocates possible solutions. The results are posted here. **Website:** www.aaafoundation.org

Advocates for Highway & Auto Safety An alliance of consumer, health, and safety groups, and insurance companies and agents working together to make America's roads safer. Encourages adoption of federal and state laws, policies, and programs that save lives and reduce injuries. Covers safety issues, federal programs, polls and reports, and state-specific issues/programs. **Website:** www.saferoads.org

Department of Transportation, U.S.A. The agency's mandate is broad and its areas of concern are many, but it is a major initiator of highway safety research and a vast repository of data on that topic. **Website:** www.dot.gov

National Safety Council (NSC) The NSC is the nation's leading advocate for safety and health. This non-governmental organization serves as an objective and impartial intermediary by bringing safety and health professionals representing industry and labor together with government, association, and public-interest representatives to form national coalitions on key safety, health, and environmental issues. The NSC library is one of the most complete safety and health information sources anywhere. The site's Driver Safety section features a host of articles and related links. Search "NSC by Topic" - driving. **Website:** www.nsc.org

🚗 **Federal Highway Administration** Provides expertise, resources, and information to continually improve the quality of our nation's highway system and its intermodal connections. Includes news on FHWA programs, highway-related legislation and regulations, and a host of articles on current highway issues. **Website:** www.fhwa.dot.gov

Vehicle-related Websites

Car magazines

🚗 *Car and Driver* Features research tools for automotive buyers and sellers, road tests, photo galleries, and multimedia and radio presentations. **Website:** www.caranddriver.com

🚗 *Edmunds* "Where smart car buyers start" Provides True Market Value (TMV®) pricing, unbiased car reviews, ratings, and expert advice to help you get a fair deal (on new and used cars). Also features online videos, auto loan calculators, ownership/maintenance articles, and much more. **Website:** www.edmund.com

🚗 *Motor Trend* "The World's #1 Automotive Authority" Includes buyer's guide, road tests, special topics, and a host of car care, driving, and equipment checklists, tips, and articles. **Website:** www.motortrend.com

🚗 *Road & Track* Comprehensive automotive reviews, road test and racing news. Includes technical reports, buyer's guide, forums. **Website:** www.roadandtrack.com

Vehicle maintenance

🚗 National Institute for Automotive Service Excellence "Certifying the Automotive Professional."The consumer portion of this site is designed to educate consumers about automotive repair. Describes the ASE Blue Seal of Excellence Program and offers a variety of Tips for Motorists (from how to communicate for better automotive service, to choosing the right repair shop or body shop, keeping your vehicle in tune with the environment, preparing your car for the various seasons, etc.). Features a ASE Blue Seal Shop locator, a women's corner, and more. **Website: www.asecert.org**

Tires

🚗 Tiresafety.com (Bridgestone/Firestone) Provides information on tire construction, size, and classification, replacement, maintenance, technology, tire terms, safety, and driving tips. You can even sign up for monthly e-mail reminders to check your tire air pressure. **Website:** www.tiresafety.com

🚗 Rubber Manufacturers Association (RMA) The national trade association for the rubber products industry. Features a downloadable section on tire maintenance and safety **Website:** www.rma.org

SUVs

🚗 The SUV Info Link Launched by Friends of the Earth "so people looking to buy a new vehicle will have all the facts about SUVs." Their interests lie in making SUVs safer and cleaner, in ensuring that perspective vehicle purchasers are educated in their choices, and in encouraging them to make the most environmentally sound decision. Includes descriptions of SUVs, comparisons with passenger cars, environmental concerns, aspects of costs, safety concerns, and other resources. **Website:** www.suv.org

Index